Medardo Rosso

Ecce puer. (1906—7). Wax over plaster, 17″ high. The Joseph H. Hirshhorn Collection, New York

Medardo Rosso

BY MARGARET SCOLARI BARR

THE MUSEUM OF MODERN ART, NEW YORK

distributed by Doubleday & Company, Inc., Garden City, N. Y.

© 1963, The Museum of Modern Art
11 West 53 Street, New York 19, N. Y.

Library of Congress Catalogue Card No. 63-19795

Printed in the U. S. A. by Capital City Press,
Montpelier, Vermont

Designed by Joseph Bourke Del Valle

This book has been produced
with the aid of a grant from
The Joseph H. Hirshhorn Foundation

ERRATA

page 22 The caption for *The Sacristan* should read:
The Sacristan. (1883). Painted plaster, 15¾" high.
Peridot Gallery, New York

page 82 The caption for the drawing *At the Café La Roche*
should read:
At the Café La Roche. Collection Dr. Gianni Mattioli,
Milan

Contents

Acknowledgments

Bringing back to life an artist who died thirty-five years ago has two things in common with the task of exhuming an artist who died in a more distant past: the attentive study of his works and of related visual material, and the appraisal of documents. Early in his study the scholar must learn to discern between source material and garbled repetitions.

In the case of an artist who died less than two generations ago there is another source, more vivid than the written page—the words of his survivors. For their lively remembrances of Medardo Rosso I wish to thank: Mario Vianello Chiodo of Venice, whose devotion to the sculptor made an indelible impression on me; Signora Tilde Rosso, widow of Francesco Rosso, Medardo's son, and, until her death in 1962, the jealous keeper of the private Rosso museum in Barzio (Valsassina) near Como; Ardengo Soffici, Rosso's foremost defender, as serious and intense in 1960 as he was when he strove effectively for Rosso's recognition in Italy from 1908 to the present; Giuseppe Prezzolini of Columbia University, editor of *La Voce* and one of the courageous organizers of the First Impressionist Exhibition in Florence (1910), who put at my disposal his archives concerning this exhibition, as well as many personal letters of Rosso's, and who also enabled me to see and to publish here the only known painting by Rosso; Giuseppe Ungaretti, one of Italy's foremost poets, for his perfect recall of Rosso's way of speaking and of the objects he collected; Knud Verlow and Christian Zervos for their impressions of Rosso in Paris; Mrs. Ida Maria Sachs the actress (affectionately known in New York by the name of Puma) who remembers Rosso from Vienna days and exclaimed of him: "Il était beau!"; Mr. and Mrs. Carlo Carrà who were "friends of the first order" in Rosso's last years in Milan; Professor Giorgio Nicodemi, recently retired editor of *L'Arte*, who knew Rosso in Milan and who afforded me un-stinting scholarly assistance, allowing me the use of his library in Milan, sending me obscure publications, and patiently answering all my letters of inquiry.

I wish to convey my appreciation to Dr. A. M. Hammacher, Director of the Rijksmuseum Kröller-Müller, Otterlo, who offered me the hospitality of the *Nederlands Kunsthistorisch Jaarboek* for my article on Medardo Rosso and his Dutch patroness Etha Fles; to Miss Agatha Verkroost, Miss Fles's adopted daughter; to Jacob van der Waals, who pursued the hunt for letters, documents, and photographs with great zeal; to Dr. Walter van Alphen de Veer and Miss Alexandrine Osterkamp for a wealth of information on the sculptor and his connections with Holland.

I am particularly grateful to Mrs. May Cippico for the firm identification and dating of the *Ecce puer*; to Dr. Luciano Caramel, the only young scholar in Italy who has done new research on Rosso and who generously shared his discoveries with me.

For investigation, documentation, assistance in procuring photographic material, and reporting references in books and periodicals I had not thought of exploring I want to thank: the late Stefano Berizzi; Rosamond Bernier, editor of *L'Oeil*; Dr. Carlo Bertelli, Sovrintendenza delle Gallerie del Lazio; Dr. Palma Bucarelli, Director, Galleria Nazionale d'Arte Moderna, Rome; Raffaele Carrieri; Giorgio Castelfranco, Gabinetto Fotografico Nazionale, Rome; Professor Cesare Fasola; Dr. Albert Elsen, Indiana University; Gino Ghiringhelli, Il Milione, Milan; Antonio Gnan, Archivi della Biennale, Venice; Ellen Joosten, Rijksmuseum Kröller-Müller, Otterlo; Bernard Karpel, Librarian, The Museum of Modern Art, New York; Sheila LaFarge, New York; Dr. Emilio Lavagnino, Sovrintendente, Gallerie del Lazio; Abram Lerner, The Hirshhorn Collection, New York; Jacques Lipchitz; Richard Lippold; Dr. Luigi Mallè, Museo Civico, Turin; Dr.

Gianni Mattioli; Nicky Mariano, Berenson Foundation, Settignano; John Mathias; John McAndrew, Wellesley College; Sibyl Moholy-Nagy, Pratt Institute; Dr. Erwin Panofsky; Danila Rosso Parravicini of Barzio, the sculptor's granddaughter; Henry Pearlman; Dr. Guido Perocco, Director, Galleria Internazionale d'Arte Moderna, Venice; John Pope Hennessy, Victoria and Albert Museum, London; Dr. M. Raumschüssel, Director, Staatliche Kunstsammlungen, Dresden; Alice Rewald; John Richardson; Helmut Ripperger, Knoedler and Co.; Gino Severini; A. James Speyer, Art Institute of Chicago; Dr. Leo Steinberg; Signora Agnes Surdi, Rome; Dr. Vittorio Viale, Director, Museo Civico, Turin; Gianni Vianello, Galleria Internazionale d'Arte Moderna, Venice; Roswitha Viollet; Lamberto Vitali; Mr. and Mrs. Harry L. Winston; Leopoldo Zorzi.

For reading the manuscript or portions of it and for making valuable suggestions I am indebted to Alfred H. Barr, Jr., John Rewald, James Thrall Soby, and Peter Selz, Director of the Medardo Rosso exhibition at the Museum of Modern Art. Because of the unflagging interest of Dr. Lucia Pallavicini, this exhibition was organized with the co-operation of the Ministry of Foreign Affairs of the Republic of Italy and the Istituto Italiano di Cultura in New York.

To Louis Pollack, who first exhibited Medardo Rosso in the United States and aided me unstintingly, I owe very special thanks.

My greatest debt is to my editor, Irene Gordon, without whose patient and skilled assistance this monograph could not have been completed.

M.S.B.
New York, March 1963

Introduction

"Medardo Rosso . . . is now, beyond a doubt, the greatest living sculptor. . . ."
GUILLAUME APOLLINAIRE, 1918

Apollinaire's unqualified superlative will charm the ears of Rosso's admirers, but it may shock those who know that during the decade before the first World War, Apollinaire, champion of Cubism, had been the sword and shield of the avant-garde.

It is true that when Apollinaire wrote his encomium of Rosso (page 64) he was referring to the recent death of Rodin, but had he forgotten Bourdelle and Maillol, sculptors of Rosso's generation? And what of Apollinaire's own contemporaries, the Cubists Archipenko, Duchamp-Villon, Lipchitz, Laurens, Picasso? What of Brancusi, Modigliani, Lehmbruck, Nadelman, and Matisse? How could Apollinaire subordinate all these sculptors, young and old, to Medardo Rosso? Yet his assertion can scarcely be ignored. He was, after all, the foremost critic of his time.

When, in 1929, Rosso's memorial exhibition was held in the Salon d'Automne, none of the reviewers, favorable or unfavorable, remarked that during the last quarter of his life Rosso had completed only one sculpture, the *Ecce puer* (frontispiece; page 57). Perhaps Apollinaire was not entirely aware that the man he proclaimed the "greatest living sculptor" in 1918 was scarcely at all a twentieth-century artist. In the second half of his career Rosso, intent on acquiring wider renown, traveled restlessly, grew eccentric in conduct and speech, and was subject to a variety of malaises. His burdens were greatly lightened by the enduring devotion of his Dutch friend, Etha Fles, and later by the generosity of his son Francesco. Yet his production was limited to variants or replicas of work done many years earlier.

Rosso's influence on other sculptors has rarely been explicit, but it has been recurrent and sometimes important. In the case of Rodin it was highly controversial. Whether Rodin owed much or little or nothing to Rosso in the final plaster version of the *Balzac*, it is evident, I think, that during the preceding half dozen years, Rosso had produced a number of sculptures more radical in their bold abstraction and freedom of form than had Rodin or, for that matter, any other European sculptor of the late nineteenth century, with the possible exception of Gauguin.

The Italian Futurists were the first twentieth-century artists to proclaim Rosso's "revolutionary importance." Boccioni, in his brilliant *Technical Manifesto of Futurist Sculpture* (1912), asserts that Medardo Rosso is "the only modern sculptor who has attempted to widen the scope of sculpture by rendering plastically the effect of environment upon the subject as well as the ties that bind it to the surrounding atmosphere." Boccioni clearly recognizes Rosso's Impressionist limitations but speaks of Rosso's "liberation of space" and concludes that the "aesthetic revolution" of Futurist sculpture originated in Rosso's experiments. Less certain is the effect of Rosso on other twentieth-century sculptors. He may well have influenced the subtle elisions and asymmetries in the modeling of certain heads by Picasso, Matisse, Brancusi, perhaps Lehmbruck, and, more recently, Manzù and other Italian sculptors of the mid-century.

Rosso's fame faded after his death, though less in Italy than in the rest of Europe; but since the second World War it has gradually risen both in his own country and internationally. For instance, five years ago no works by Rosso were known to be in American collections; now there are some twenty, of which three are in the Museum of Modern Art.

Why does Rosso interest us now? Such pieces of the early 1890's as the extraordinary *Conversation in the Garden* (page 41), the *Bookmaker* (page 44), the *Man Reading* (page 45), are astonishing for their date, and remain aesthetically fascinating. Historically these are the very works which anticipate Rodin's *Balzac*, the first great monumental Expressionist sculpture. The reappraisal of Rosso is perhaps related to the revival of enthusiasm for Rodin, though Rodin's looming figure will not again obscure Rosso's fame.

Rosso's reputation, like Rodin's, suffered for a quarter of a century from the label Impressionist; in recent years both the term and the style itself have been restored to honor, partly by postwar avant-garde painters in whose work Impressionism is sometimes mingled with Expressionism and abstraction. He was indeed an Impressionist in so far as his medium would permit. Impatient with the limitations of sculpture, he never tried consciously to emulate the Impressionist painters, yet, like them, he was passionately interested in light and, like them, he wanted to fuse his subjects with the air, the sun, the haze, the gaslight, and the color in which they were steeped. This is what he meant when he said: "Nothing is material in space," or "We are nothing but a play of light."

Boccioni noted with admiration Rosso's attempt to fuse his figures with visible, yet abstract, fragments of their surroundings, as in *Baby Chewing Bread* (page 39), *Lady with a Veil* (page 42), *Madame Noblet* (page 52). The results in their delicate *sfumato* effects and wild environmental tatters are as different from the clarity and solidity of Maillol and Brancusi as they are from the academic statuary of Rosso's contemporaries of the 1890's.

We like Rosso's sculpture, too, because of its informality and impetuous spontaneity, just as we tend to prefer Bernini's or Canova's *bozzetti* to their highly finished marbles. Several of Rosso's sculptures must have seemed mere sketches to his contemporaries and may have been dismissed as such. But they are not sketches by intention, nor are they studies; they are final.

Unlike Rodin and the Salon sculptors, Rosso belligerently denied the past. To him the revered works of the Greeks and Romans were "nothing but paperweights." A quarter century before the Futurist Marinetti disparaged the *Victory of Samothrace*, Rosso tweaked the beard of Michelangelo's *Moses* and had literally turned his back on Renaissance Florence. Yet his *Little Girl Laughing* (page 33), his *Sick Boy* (page 40), and his *Petite rieuse* (page 35), suggest certain portrait heads of the Quattrocento or even the soft waxen quality of Praxitelean marbles.

Rosso was a realist somewhat in the sense that the Impressionists were realists; he depended initially on his sensations of the visible world. He was often a realist, too, in his subject matter, a humanitarian realist as Daumier and Zola were —Daumier who probably influenced him, and Zola who bought his *Concierge* (page 24). The overt humor of a few early pieces, the sentiment or pathos of some of his later heads may strike us as too obvious, but at a time when the "new realism" and the "new humanism" are again catchwords, if not passwords, Rosso's sculpture has some special relevance.

Yet the relevance seems topical, even a little specious, when we contemplate the mysterious heads and faces of women half merged in a visible, palpable ambiance and study the strange figures of men which seem to grow out of the earth like tree trunks with spreading roots. Rosso's art is complex, ambiguous, his vision poetic as much as objective. "The eye," he said, "is a second light."

Medardo Rosso

EARLY YEARS, FIRST INFLUENCES

Medardo Rosso was born in 1858 in Turin, which then, before the unification of Italy, was the capital of the kingdom of Sardinia. His father, handsome and something of a philanderer, was the proud stationmaster of the Turin-Genoa line and later, in 1859, dispatched Piedmontese troops and Garibaldini in the turmoil of the Risorgimento. Medardo, the youngest of three children, was probably his mother's favorite, for his attachment to her provides the best key to his character, to the yearning sentiment that underlies many of his works, and to the unusual trajectory of his life. He received a cursory education and displayed at an early age a rebelliousness that, far from diminishing with maturity, became somehow his banner, so that when his own son was born in 1885, he insisted on registering him with the names Francesco, Evviva (hurrah), Ribelle (rebel).

When Medardo was twelve, the family moved to Milan. As a schoolboy he often managed to escape to the workshop of a stonecutter, returning in the evening in a telltale, dusty disarray. A friend who stayed with the Rosso family in 1872 remembered that the young boy quarreled with his father and leaned upon his mother for love and protection. By late adolescence he had forced his family to accept the fact that he would not work in the railroads and that he intended to be an artist.[1]

In 1879 he was compelled to enlist in the place of his weakling brother. As his troop train passed through Florence on the way to Rome, he covered his eyes to avoid the sight of the city that had cradled the Renaissance, which he already abhorred. In Rome he went to see Michelangelo's *Moses*, whose beard he compared to "a mass of Neapolitan spaghetti."

Thirty-six months in the new army of the kingdom of Italy left an indelible scar; constantly recalcitrant, Rosso found discipline unendurable. Some of his officers showed tolerance and understanding by allowing him to paint their portraits and alleviating the menial tasks that would have been his lot. In retrospect, Rosso's experience as a private was not altogether unfortunate since it brought him new friends;[2] artistically, too, it bore fruit, because when he had no money for paints and canvases, he began to model in clay.[3] Such was his delight with this medium that, when mustered out of the service, he enrolled in the Brera Academy in Milan for courses in anatomy and sculpture.

Rosso soon realized that his true masters were not at the Academy. The teaching, from mannequins and casts, was unimaginative and boring. The models in life classes were all male. Other artists, older than he, had turned against dry classicism and were pursuing nature according to their own lights. Possibly even before his military service he may have been acquainted with the paintings of Daniele Ranzoni (1843–1889) and of Tranquillo Cremona (1837–1878), who favored suave light effects, a tremulous description of forms dissolved in their surrounding air, and a rather obvious palette of cool and warm colors.[4] These two men belonged to the Milanese movement known as the *Scapigliatura* (literally, Dishevelment), which, in the sixties, in a belated flowering of sentimental, anecdotal romanticism, established a stand against both the last waves of neo-classicism and the earnest equilibrium and virtue of the overwhelmingly dominant Milanese novelist and poet Alessandro Manzoni.[5] A sculptor, too, belonged to this group of rebels who effervesced in a vacuum because no one knew they existed or cared that they were rebelling: Giuseppe Grandi (1843–1894) who, after training at the Brera, had acquired through Odoardo Tabacchi (1831–1905) a pictorial rather

Medardo Rosso

than a slick manner of modeling, as well as an informal, spirited realism (*verismo*). Grandi did many popular genre statuettes with quaint titles (page 66), but he also received important commissions for public monuments, one of which elicited from a critic the remark that it was "chiseled with a brush, in fact, with the brush of Tiepolo." At the time, the notion of the equivalence and interchangeability of the arts was highly popular in intellectual circles, and its effects were to be felt throughout Europe up to the threshold of the twentieth century, when the word synesthesia was much in fashion. To write pictorially or musically, to compose a tone poem, to paint in sculpture, to make music in painting was the aim of many artists of the second half of the nineteenth century, all of whom considered tone to be the binding element among the arts.[6]

Formative also for Rosso were Baudelaire's remarks about sculpture which, according to Louis Piérard, he happened to see while he was in the army.[7] The pertinent passage reads as follows:

The origin of sculpture is lost in the mists of time; thus it is a *Carib* art.

We find, in fact, that all races bring real skill to the carving of fetishes long before they embark upon the art of painting, which is an art involving profound thought and one whose enjoyment demands a particular initiation.

Sculpture comes much closer to nature, and that is why even today our peasants, who are enchanted by the sight of an ingeniously-turned fragment of wood or stone, will nevertheless remain unmoved in front of the most beautiful painting. Here we have a singular mystery which is quite beyond human solving.

Sculpture has several disadvantages which are a necessary consequence of its means and materials. Though as brutal and positive as nature herself, it has at the same time a certain vagueness and ambiguity, because it exhibits too many surfaces at once. It is in vain that the sculptor forces himself to take up a unique point of view, for the spectator who moves around the figure can choose a hundred different points of view, except for the right one, and it often happens that a chance trick of the light, an effect of the lamp, may discover a beauty which is not at all the one the artist had in mind—and this is a humiliating thing for him. A picture, however, is only what it wants to be; there is no other way of looking at it than on its own terms. Painting has but one point of view; it is exclusive and absolute, and therefore the painter's expression is much more forceful.[8]

The words *"Carib* art" for sculpture in the round, the contempt for statues that could be turned on their stands and contemplated from every angle, the ideal of the unique point of view, were to haunt Rosso throughout his life, for Bau-

months, from May 3, 1882, to March 29, 1883, when he was expelled because he had laid hands on a fellow student who refused to sign a petition he was circulating in an effort to obtain live models of women and children besides those of men.

LEFT: *The Hooligan.* (1882). Bronze, 9 1/2" high
Galleria d'Arte Moderna, Rome

BELOW: *Unemployed Singer.* (1882). Bronze, 11 1/2" high
Galleria d'Arte Moderna, Rome

delaire's expressions recur in the many recorded monologues about his beliefs and achievements.

What did Rosso actually know about French Impressionism before his first trip to Paris in 1884? Milanese critics did write about it, and Diego Martelli, Degas' friend, had given a lecture on Impressionism in Leghorn in 1879, which was published in Florence in 1880. But what are words without visual evidence? Photographs were rare, and dully reproduced. In any case, Rosso read little. However, in cafés or at artists' gatherings, he came to know Vittore Grubicy de Dragon (1851—1920), who had begun his career as a picture dealer and had traveled extensively throughout Europe.[9] Only seven years older than Rosso, alert, aglow, full of stories of magically exciting cities, of artists conversing and working toward common goals, he must have set fire to the imagination of the young sculptor and opened his horizons not only through conversation but by showing him reproductions, prints, or actual works by the most advanced painters of Paris hitherto unknown to him in his restricted and rather provincial milieu.[10]

Rosso's mind must have been in a ferment. He endured the teachings of the Academy for eleven

Kiss Under the Lamppost. (1882)
Bronze, 18 7/8" high including base
Collection Jack Berizzi, New York

FIRST MILAN PERIOD

Rosso's earliest sculpture, *The Hooligan*[11] (page 12), was executed either in the army or, more probably, in the early Brera days.[12] Supposedly a portrait of the sculptor Rescaldani, its original title was *Il fumatore* (*The Smoker*) because in the earliest version a clay pipe was stuck in the flaring right-hand corner of the lips. The smoke rising to the right eye accounts for its lowered lid; the asymmetrical treatment of the two sides of the face is curiously prophetic of the later devices that Rosso was to use in his maturity.

Close to the genre statuettes[13] of Grandi, both in pictorial modeling and in subject, is the small *Unemployed Singer*,[14] 1882 (page 12), which, despite the title, is a self-portrait of the artist in his shabby winter coat. The legs, modeled separately, present a "hole"; never again did he render the voids formed by the human limbs because he realized that there were no voids in nature, only light and air.

Kiss Under the Lamppost,[15] also 1882 (above), in its original version had had a miniature street light that shone on the group from above, but in any light the movement of the two small protagonists is telling: the male eager, the female partially resisting as she is pressed against the lamppost, and partially yielding as the lower portion of her body slips forward from waist to out-stretched foot. No unnecessary detail detracts from the nebulous impression of an embrace seen from afar in the shadows of the street at night. Rosso's photographic eye enabled him to render in his studio what he had seized in a fleeting instant as he walked through the city.

The *Garibaldino*,[16] 1882 (page 15), nearly life-size, is more realistic and descriptive not only because of the recognizable red cap and tassel, but because the tension of the face still caked with the dust of battle is explicitly stated in the sideways glance, the tightened cheek muscles, and the compressed lips concealed by a drooping mustache; it is an indignant evocation. Twelve years after the unification of Italy, Garibaldi's heroic veterans were already forgotten in the settled calm of the kingdom of Italy, which they had helped to forge.[17] Through this head, Rosso rose to their defense. The cause of the downtrodden was always his, not only because he personally felt deprived of love, protection, and admiration, but because he was a man of his time. The sentimental, humanitarian attitude of the late nineteenth century, so evident in the pathos of Picasso's earliest works, manifested itself in a dolorous sympathy for the oppressed, the poor, the sick. It was a subjective leaning that implied no active sense of social duty—save perhaps the passing of a few coins to beggars. Hand in hand with this posture of commiseration went a merciless, self-righteous pruriency for the more symbolic forms of vice: the prostitute, the drinker, the exploiter of the poor or the credulous. Rosso's subjects, as well as certain of his forced and gratuitous titles, reflect this *fin-de-siècle* point of view.

His next work, in a lighter vein, represents a laughing, sly adolescent in a soft cap (page 15). Entitled *Lo scugnizzo (Street Boy)*,[18] 1882, he renamed it *Gavroche* after he went to France. He made many casts of it, varying the expression by changing the angle of the head, but in all versions it has the perky vivacity of genre sculpture then much in vogue in Italy. It is, as a matter of fact, the portrait of his young studio helper Bustelli, laughing as he watched an improvised puppet show with other children of the neighborhood. Rosso's collection of puppets appears in the photograph he sent Baldassare Surdi in 1883 or early in 1884.[19]

Still in 1882 he executed a funerary monument that was lost when the Gentilino cemetery was abolished to make room for the expanding city of Milan. It exists in a single photograph taken at the plaster stage, which leads one to wonder whether it ever was cast in bronze. Called *The Last Kiss*[20] (page 16), it represents a young bare-foot girl prone on the ground leaning over a wire grating that she is trying to touch with her lips. The unrestrained sentimentalism of the subject calls to mind the most anxiously touching creations of the masters of the *Scapigliatura*. The head, arms, and feet are delicately treated, but the rippling skirt seems, in the photograph, to be a lifeless jumble of plaster.

These works, and perhaps one or two more, were done while Rosso was at the Academy, and some were exhibited in the Vercesi Gallery in Milan. Then, most fortunately, in April 1883, less than a month after his expulsion, Rosso was invited to exhibit at the Esposizione di Belle Arti in Rome. He showed *The Hooligan, Street Boy, Unemployed Singer*, and a fourth work listed as *In esplorazione*, which might be the *Garibaldino* renamed for the occasion. Though he could hardly afford the train trip, Rosso traveled down to Rome; when he could not pay for a room, he slept under the vaults of the Colosseum. At the exhibition he fell into conversation with a painter, Baldassare Surdi, who had many connections in Rome and entertained in his incomparable studio in the Villa Borghese. One day, on an impulse, Rosso painted Surdi's portrait, and this, for the moment, is the only known canvas by his hand (page 17).[21] It is a dark picture in a gamut of muffled tans and browns hardly relieved by the whitish frame of the chair and its red upholstery. The head, strongly modeled in chiaroscuro, reveals a structural assurance that is surprisingly lacking in the hands. This sober portrait of a nineteenth-century gentleman does not suggest that Rosso was a colorist; he spoke of color, though never of specific colors, he read color into

Garibaldino. (1882). Bronze, 12 1/2" high
Whereabouts unknown

Gavroche. (1882). Bronze, 9 1/4" high
Galleria d'Arte Moderna, Rome

his sculptures, he liked to install them close to paintings so that they could receive reflected color. But he did not crave to manipulate and mix the wealth of colors that were by then so easily available to painters. He could say all he wanted by light and shadow. And besides, the manual feeling of clay and the taxing processes of sculpture gave him greater satisfaction.

Pleased with his portrait, Baldassare Surdi spoke with enthusiasm about his young protégé to the critic de Horatiis who interviewed him and wrote a long piece about him, proclaiming him to be "true manna for Italian art."[22] Surdi forwarded the clipping to Milan and Rosso thanked him with youthful ebullience:

Milan 27 April 1883

Dearest Sig. Surdi,

You cannot imagine what an effect Sig. D'Orazio's [sic] article had on me, and the little head reproduced, for which I sincerely congratulate Sig.

Foli [obviously the photographer]. I cannot express the happiness and emotion that all these things [gave me], and whom should I thank but you who did so much to arrange that these things should be put in your paper, thus opening for me such a fine artistic road and honoring me in the eyes of the world. I confess that I would not be able to express to you the pleasure I felt at that moment—I wept, I sang, I danced, then I had to leave the studio and go for a walk because I could no longer manage to work. One friend wanted me here, another there—in a word, it was something to see. I looked, I read, and read again, but I didn't think it was for me—to have really reached the point I had so intensely desired! Ah yes, I promise you, neither you nor Sig. D'Orazio will need to wait long, because I shall want truly to confirm his words with something worth while. But apart from this, I should like to be near you, to be able to give you a fine big kiss. For I shall never be able to prove to you, no matter what I do—because the obligation I feel toward you is too too great. . . . Do you remember the day I met you and I told you my affairs and my troubles?

The Last Kiss. (1882). Plaster. Destroyed

Portrait of Baldassare Surdi. (1883). Oil on canvas,
31 1/4 x 22 3/4″. Collection Mrs. Agnes Surdi, Rome

Now, how can I really, with what you have done for me, speak differently? How can I—how could I?

The devotion I feel for you, you cannot imagine it, and this is saying little in consideration of what I have suffered for art. I am only happy to be a friend and to have a sincere and loyal friend, and I would be even happier if at this moment I could embrace you as I feel like doing.

Stay fond of me, write to me, and believe me most cordially if you will permit, your very affectionate friend

Medardo Rosso

P.S. I am reading again and I cannot believe that that beautiful article should be about me. It is too much, really.

This is the earliest Rosso letter we know and the only extant one he ever dated. The handwrit-

ing is small, slanted, and precise (page 80). Each sentence has a fairly logical structure. There are few mistakes in spelling. It is written in acceptable Italian, not in dialect or mixed languages as are his many letters written after 1906.[23] As a gesture of gratitude, Rosso also sent Surdi a photograph of the *Last Kiss* and one of his studio in Milan, in which he had arranged most of his works (page 18).[24] Halfway through the time exposure, Rosso himself entered the picture, at the left: his intense face, tousled hair, and slight, drooping mustache are the clearest record of his appearance at twenty-five.

Under the stimulus of his success in Rome he worked a great deal in the ensuing months, pursuing several lines of investigation at once in order to obtain more vivid atmospheric effects in sculpture. If we assumed that the photograph he mailed Surdi contained all his works up to the moment of sending except for the *Last Kiss* (which he mailed separately), it is not unreasonable to surmise that the *Mother and Child Sleeping* (page 19) is the worth-while work he half-promised in his letter from Milan, the work that would prove to his new Roman friends that they had not put their faith in him in vain. He chose a subject pleasing to others, and to which he himself was singularly responsive, for he, an agnostic, invested the theme of mother love with truly religious connotations. Not to be ignored in this psycho-logical context is the figurine, now lost, at the extreme right in the Surdi photograph, of a mother bending low to suckle her child.

This *Mother and Child Sleeping*,[25] 1883, a work recently rediscovered,[26] is the first of Rosso's three compositions of women holding infants. It contains in embryo some elements that, after further searchings, were to become salient in Rosso's mature work: first, and most importantly, it can be seen only from the front, for the admirable bronze cast is a relatively light concave shell; secondly, the pictorial modeling, more evident in the head of the baby, depends on correct lighting; and finally, the inventive handling of the

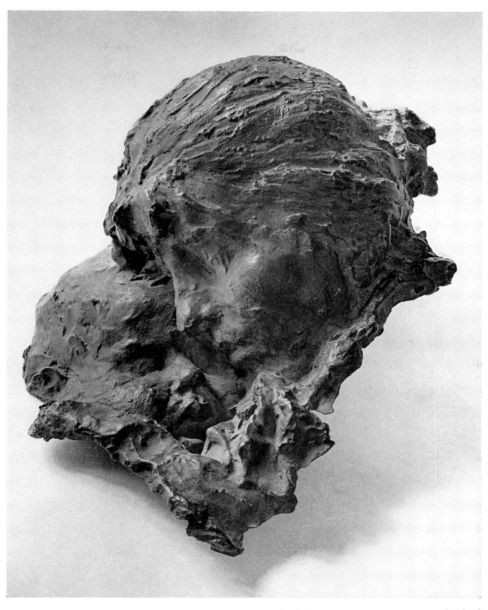

Mother and Child Sleeping. (1883). Bronze, 13 7/8" high
Collection Cesare Fasola, Bagno a Ripoli (Florence)

OPPOSITE: Rosso's studio in Milan, 1883
From left to right: *The Procuress* (with the word *fine*—
the end—on its rough base), *The Hooligan, Unemployed
Singer, Gavroche, The Hooligan* (again), *Gavroche* (in
another cast), *Garibaldino* (in bronze) or some other sad
male head with real cloth draped around the neck, *Mother
and Child Sleeping, Kiss Under the Lamppost,* a statuette
of a mother suckling her child (*not* Rosso's version of the
Medici *Madonna*). High up, attached to the wall, is a plaster cast of a sly hag with a wide black hat clapped on her
head for fun. Pinned on to the sackcloth that is arranged
as a sort of backdrop are some puppets that hinder the
easy reading of the sculpture but bring to mind the laugh-
ter of the *Gavroche.* Rosso appears at the left, partially
hidden by the screen.

eyes appears as the first announcement of his brilliant late solutions. Nevertheless, there are still some tactile passages, for the human hand could recognize the mother's straight hair gathered in a knot at the back, her nose, and her mouth, as well as the bulging forehead, nose, and wide-open mouth of the child.

Rosso knew that he could go much further, and he began to seek out in the faces of the aged the actual "in-and-out of space," the fractures of surface, that the sleek features of the young did not visually offer. So he fell back on the humble old people who were fixtures in his neighborhood and whom he saw anew with a heightened awareness.

Because artists always like their last work best, the head called *The Procuress*[27] (below) is featured prominently at the left in the Surdi photograph, with the word *fine* (the end) boldly written on the improvised pedestal. The end of what? the end of life that begins with babyhood, passes through the beauty of young mothers, and comes to a close in the ghastly wrinkles and toothless-

Mr. Faust. (1883). Wax over plaster, 14" high
Rosso Museum, Barzio

The Procuress. (1883). Wax over plaster, 14" high
Galleria d'Arte Moderna, Rome

ness of this realistic head weirdly echoed, in the same photograph, by the plaster head with a black hat that floats like a ghost high on the wall.[28]

The male companion piece to the *Procuress* is *Mr. Faust*[29] (above), in reality the husband of Rosso's *portinaia* at 3, Via Montebello, who was within the year to become the model for his admirable *Concierge* (page 24). *The Procuress* and *Mr. Faust*, both of them realistic to the point of caricature, justifiable only by the ideals of Italian *verismo*, should be considered experimental works, for what interested Rosso at this stage were the ridges and gullies of faces eroded by time. He needed to search out in visible reality the projections and recessions he was on the verge of redisposing arbitrarily to make his creations vibrate in the vivifying shimmer of light.

The Procuress is Rosso's earliest extant sculpture in wax. There were no immediate precedents for this medium in nineteenth-century Italy. Canova's "inventions," often so close to Rosso's work, were in plaster or pale terracotta; the polychrome crèche statuettes of Naples and Sicily were in painted terracotta or in wood; but Rosso's contemporaries in northern Italy all worked in marble or bronze. As Rosso's sculptures before the *Procuress* are known to us only in bronze or plaster, it is not unreasonable to suspect that while preparing to cast the head by the cire-perdue method, he stopped short because he may have found that wax rendered to perfection the bloodless transparencies and flabby folds of the old woman's face.

Rosso never made preparatory drawings but invented directly in clay. From the clay he made a *modello* or working model in plaster, then he made a negative mold from which he cast either in bronze or again in plaster, thereby obtaining a duplicate of his original *modello*; this he coated with wax, varying many details in each of his new versions.[30]

Although as a boy he had worked for a stone-cutter, Rosso never carved in marble; he did not share Michelangelo's belief that a form should be searched out in the block by "taking away." Clay was his medium, and his fingers, even more than the spatula, were his tools. He often said that he wanted the material of his sculptures to pass unnoticed because they were meant to blend with the "unity" of the world that surrounded them. The twentieth-century theory that a sculptor with true artistic integrity should "be faithful to his material" left him untouched.

Portrait of the Artist's Mother on Her Deathbed. (1884). Drawing. Rosso Museum, Barzio

EMERGENCE OF A PERSONAL STYLE

It is at this moment, in the second half of 1883 and the beginning of 1884, that Rosso evolves a style of his own which is far more than a retort to Baudelaire's invectives against "circumambulatable" sculpture. The painter in him comes to the fore as he invents devices to render in clay the vagueness of atmospheric envelopment that seems to dematerialize tangible forms. Again, as a painter, he grasps the fact that protrusions and hollows in sculpture can be made to play a double game: "What's behind comes forward and what's in front goes backward,"[31] he used to say—an ex- traordinary discovery upon which so much twentieth-century sculpture is predicated. As he softens his contours and crumbles his forms to marry them into their aura, he sees the shadows they cast as cohesive and essential to them. The many liberties he takes so suddenly with conventional sculpture are facilitated for him by the *non finito* passages in Michelangelo's work and by the taste, matured in the Romantic period, for the sketchy, fresh, impetuous, and direct artistic creation.

The Sacristan,[32] of 1883 (below), marks the sudden maturing of Rosso the sculptor and, in a

The Sacristan. (1883). Bronze, 14 1/2" high. The Joseph H. Hirshhorn Collection, New York

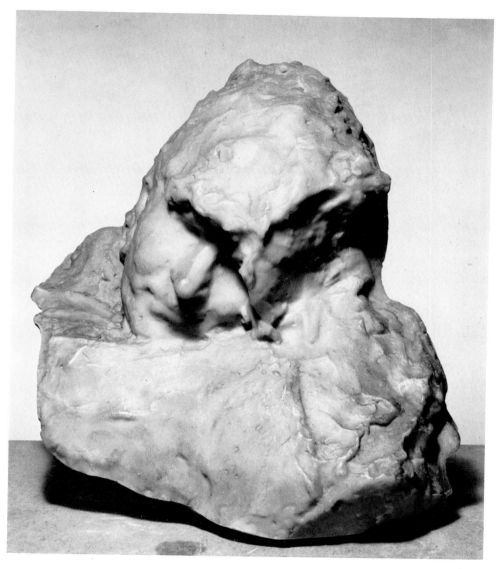

The Flesh of Others. (1883). Wax over plaster, 12" high. Whereabouts unknown

way, the resurgence of his painterly vision. His clay takes on a soft, modulated, nacreous quality in which passages of light and shadow glide in *sfumato* transitions or come up sharply in light-catching revelatory ridges like a white scumbling nervously laid upon a transparent glaze. *The Sacristan* is not a caricature; nothing anecdotal mars the compassionate interpretation of the head as —deeply bowed—it casts its shadow on a neutral background, while the alcoholic nose is handled with such sensitive discretion that it merely serves

as a guide to the tragic cavities of the eye and mouth, all seen in the still blue-gray air of stale church incense.

As if glancing back to the *Mother and Child Sleeping,* Rosso realized that the problem now was to apply the same principles to younger, smoother faces. He met the challenge with the *Flesh of Others,*[33] 1883 (above). The strong nose and heavy features of a woman in her thirties called for many gradual surface transitions, which he overshadowed by a heavy cap of hair as he

Concierge. (1883). Wax over plaster, 14 1/2″ high. The Museum of Modern Art, New York
(Mrs. Wendell T. Bush Fund)

drew up billowing bedclothes to conceal the neck bent sharply to the right. The analogy of the wistful pose to that of Michelangelo's *Madonna* in the Medici Chapel is inescapable, and Rosso was conscious of it; in the Salon d'Automne of 1904, he installed the *Flesh of Others* beside his small copy of the Medici *Madonna*, inclination echoing inclination.[34] No irreverence was implied, for his head of a Milanese prostitute has none of the mercilessness of Degas and Lautrec—it is an image of melancholy.[35]

Close to the *Sacristan* but more daring is the *Concierge*,[36] 1883—84 (page 24), a portrait of his old doorkeeper, rendered with warm sympathy, without the pedantry of wrinkles but rather with an attentive notation of the empty shrinking and sagging of old age. The sense of irascible senility is conveyed by the hollow temple, the ridge of the frowning brow, the pendulous nostril, the long upper lip, the compressed mouth that begrudges a single gracious word. Intensely pictorial, its fractured surfaces reveal the most intuitive knowledge of the effects of chiaroscuro.

The Concierge may be related to one of the figures in a large group that Rosso modeled in 1883—84[37] entitled *Impression in an Omnibus*.[38] Smashed on its way to Venice for the exhibition of 1887, it survives in poor photographs that make it hard to gauge the size and to understand whether it was a wax or merely a plaster (below). From right to left there were: a bowed old woman (the concierge?), a drunk, a genial housewife with a kerchief tied under her chin (whom Rosso called the *Marchande de légumes*), a young brooding girl in a tight toque (the *Maestrina*), and a fifth figure that is hard to decipher. The analogy to Daumier's characterizations of train passengers is evident.[39] Rosso desperately regretted the loss of this ambitious work and attempted to duplicate it in later years.[40] When he met Degas, perhaps in 1884 but much more probably after 1889 at Henri Rouart's, he showed him a photograph of it, and Degas took it to be a painting rather than a sculpture. Rosso had an acute awareness of peripheral vision and used it here with acumen, silhouetting the heads and shoulders of his protagonists against the bright light of the bus window, letting their garments merge indefinitely, and handling the figures at the extreme right and left in two differing softer focuses.

Impression in an Omnibus. (1883—84). Destroyed

In 1884, probably in the spring, Rosso became possessed with the wish to go to Paris. Tradition has it that he worked as a laborer to scrape together the price of his ticket,[41] and that he ventured forth without a plan, without an introduction, in the belief that he could make a name for himself in what he imagined to be the liberal, cosmopolitan city where daring artists worked in new ways and where an enlightened public was sympathetic to their efforts. Perhaps rumors had reached Milan that in Paris many artists, disgusted with the jury of the Salon, were on the point of organizing a new system of free exhibition—the Indépendants—where anyone could show without the censorship of a jury of admission and without the invidious accolade of "recompenses" or prizes. It may well be that he embarked on his momentous journey with the intention of entering his sculptures in the Indépendants, and that because of his impractical bent, he somehow bungled his chances.

Whatever his plans may have been, he arrived in Paris with twenty-seven lire in his pocket, and spent his first night at the Grand Hôtel, only to seek refuge within a day under the back stairs of a squalid rooming house in the slums near the Place de la République. In reminiscing, he perhaps concealed the loneliness and terror the great city had held for a young foreigner with no contacts and no money. He roamed, he tried to sell, he hunted for odd jobs to keep alive. There is no knowing whether he ever entered the Louvre, whether he saw the Manet memorial show, whether he visited the Salon or even the Indépendants, where he might have seen the work of Redon and Signac and Seurat's great *Baignade*. Perhaps deterred by the price of admission, he limited himself to dealers' galleries. In the confused record filtered through his son's memory,[42] he "refreshed himself" by going to the shop of *père* Thomas on the Boulevard Malesherbes[43] and to the fashionable Galeries Georges Petit on the Rue de Sèze whose hallowed portals he was willing to cross perhaps because he knew that one of his countrymen, the charming Giuseppe de Nittis, had been one of its founders in 1882.[44] Just around the corner on the Boulevard de la Madeleine, at Durand-Ruel's, he could have seen the work of all the important Impressionist painters. Interesting though it may be to guess at Rosso's wanderings in his first Paris visit, one essential fact remains: he found work at Dalou's as a studio assistant and, in the course of his duties, he met Rodin. In reminiscing to his son, he was to say that Rodin was working there in an equally humble role. But Rosso's memory was playing him false, obscured as it was by his bitterness after the emergence of Rodin's *Balzac*.[45] In truth, by 1884, Rodin had finished Dalou's portrait bust, had just won the competition for the *Burghers of Calais*, and since 1880 had been working on the commission for the *Gates of Hell*. So Rosso, the unknown Italian, met and conversed with two of the most successful sculptors in the art capital of the world. At twenty-seven, full of bounce and self-confidence and with the physique of a giant, he was not awed but saw as in a mirage what he, too, in time might become.

He knew he was on the right path and was convinced that his work could measure up and, in fact, surpass that of these august masters. With dreams of glory but empty pockets he went back to Milan.[46]

SECOND MILAN PERIOD, NOVEMBER 1884–SPRING 1889

Rosso's mother died in Milan on November 11, 1884; shortly after he fell into a long despondence.[47] He had made a life-size drawing of her on her deathbed[48] (page 21), and in later life, he always spoke of her lovingly but refused to utter the name of his father and elder brother against whom he harbored obscure grudges.[49] This bereavement had on Rosso, so hypersensitive, so

The Golden Age. (1886). Wax over plaster, 17″ high. Galleria d'Arte Moderna, Rome

uncertain yet hopeful, the searing effect of the loss through death of his sole support. Overwhelming waves of tenderness and nostalgia transported him as he composed his impressions of mothers and infants, of children enchanted at the dawn of life or crushed by adversity. Women, too, he henceforth beheld protectively, with a gentle feeling of blessing.

As if bogged down by despair, he created no new sculptures in 1885. On the eleventh of April he married Giuditta Pozzi, perhaps in the illusion that she could fill the gap his mother had left. But the marriage did not go well; dogged by want, the young couple had many disagreements from the very start, and their situation was by no means improved by the birth of their son Francesco. The mirage of Paris was kept alive in Rosso's mind by notices he received when works of his were

shown in the Salon or at the Indépendants.[50]

In 1886, after a year of lying fallow, he began to work again. He did a bust for the grave of Carlo Carabelli,[51] a merchant from whom he bought his plaster. In this, as in the later funerary bust of Filippo Filippi, a flange of bronze binds the head to the shoulder to create a sense of pictorial environment. The modeling, less free than in the *Concierge* though logical in a portrait, does seem a lapse into more conventional handling and is not dissimilar in forceful characterization from the male busts by Rodin which Rosso would have seen in 1884.

At last with *Golden Age*,[52] 1886 (above), he hit his stride again. The two tightly intermingled heads represent his wife and son.[53] The young mother kisses the baby so hard that her nose and mouth blend into his cheek and chin. His mouth is wide open, his eyes somewhat contracted but not closed. The mother's emaciated arm and long fleshless hand sustain the infant's head, her thumb sinks deeply into his chubby cheek. The psychological implications are ambiguous because it is hard to understand whether, as one critic has suggested, the child is frightened by the violence and compression of the mother's embrace or whether her enveloping contact is comforting him after a long spell of weeping. In the early version, an irregular margin of plaster establishes an atmospheric background behind the mother's pointed chignon and the head of the child; in later versions only a small indefinite projection appears between the two heads to sustain the illusion, quite apparent in the free modeling, that all is seen within surrounding veils of air.

The second International Exhibition (not yet called Biennale) was held in Venice in 1887. Rosso went there, and with dogged insistence compelled the acceptance of his four entries; the fifth, *Omnibus*, was smashed in transit. He had selected three of his most advanced works—*The Sacristan, The Concierge, Golden Age*—and his veristic *Procuress*, under the title *Fine*.[54] The Venice officials were not to forget his arrogance and did not admit him again until 1914.

Four other funerary monuments belong in these years: one to a Signor Trebini, not to be found in the Milan Cimitero Monumentale; one surprisingly conventional one, obviously commissioned, to Elisa Rognoni Faini[55] (page 69); one to Vincenzo Brusco Onnis (page 68), a comrade of Mazzini, dated on the urn 1888;[56] and one, 1889, to the music critic Filippo Filippi,[57] a friend of Rosso's. The two male busts, though obviously excellent likenesses, are modeled with quick rough impetus and with asymmetrical solutions, especially in the handling of the mouth and nose, softly pushed to one side to force the perspective of a three-quarter point of view; the plastic aspects of the back of the head are ignored. The tapering pedestals of the busts are elaborate, and while there is no evidence that the base of the *Brusco Onnis* is by Rosso, the one of the *Filippo Filippi* is.[58] Its complicated, somewhat illegible symbolism consisting of wispy inspirational figures and the sheet of a song with words and notes presents echoes of Art Nouveau that, surprisingly enough, are unique in Rosso's oeuvre.

OPPOSITE: *Child at the Breast.* (1889). Bronze, 20 1/2" high. Galleria d'Arte Moderna, Rome

SECOND PARIS PERIOD, 1889—1897

Years later Rosso seems to have said that he was recalled to Paris for the Exposition Universelle of 1889.[59] By whom would he have been recalled? Perhaps by Gastone Pesce? We do not know. Rosso was an exceptionally secretive man; he not only concealed important facts that might have put him in a bad light but even the most irrelevant and casual things. Certainly in reminiscing either to his son or to friends, he never revealed the true reasons that led him to desert his wife and son. He may have decided to make a quick trip to Paris to enter some sculptures in the Exposition, fully intending to go back to Milan.[60] It is perhaps not too far-fetched to imagine that he arrived penniless in the *ville lumière* (graced now by its brand-new landmark, the Eiffel Tower), that he was forced to live in miserable circumstances, that he fell ill, slowly recuperated, and began to work again in fairly acceptable circumstances. Always improvident, impractical, thinking of nothing but his art, he may have postponed his return from month to month hoping that in France he might

Child at the Breast. (1889). Bronze, 15″ high
Peridot Gallery, New York

obtain the recognition and success that had been denied him in the past four years in Milan. No matter in what frame of mind and with what intentions he left Milan, by June 26, 1889, he was in Paris[61] where he had the satisfaction of seeing five of his works exhibited in the Exposition Universelle.[62] By September, Emile Zola had bought his *Concierge*.[63]

Related to the year 1889 is Rosso's third and last mother-and-child composition, *Child at the Breast*[64] (left). The work represents a mother suckling her baby as she looks down at it with a proud smile that is all the more touching because she is a plain woman with high cheekbones, deep-set eyes, and a long pointed nose; the features of the baby are hard to seize in the agitated billows that separate it from the mother's head. Rosso himself must have realized in the course of time that it was impossible to read the two heads in the same light, so in later casts he cut away the head of the mother (above).[65]

Also dated 1889 is *Man in the Hospital*[66] (page 31), a small but most sensitive work. Not long after his arrival, perhaps from sheer starvation,[67] Rosso fell ill and was forced to seek refuge in the Lariboisière Hospital.[68] It is here that he beheld the broken old man in a heavy robe sitting in a low armchair. The sight impressed itself upon his retina and upon his tender heart. As soon as he was released he created with a few assured strokes of thumb and spatula this image of taciturn desolation. As in the *Concierge*, Rosso is dealing with essentials nobly stated; not a trace remains of the descriptive genre aspects of his early works.

This illness of Rosso's was a blessing in disguise, for it brought him in contact with Henri Rouart, one of the most courageous and adventurous collectors of the time. Louis Rouart, Henri's son, reminisced about the past with his sister-in-law, Mme Ernest Rouart (Julie Manet), who wrote down his memories. This is what he recalled about Rosso:[69]

Every day my father [Henri] passed by the shop of a little picture dealer named Thomas opposite the church of St.-Augustin. One day, attracted by a sculpture, he went in to ask the name of its author. Thomas told him that it was by a poor Italian sculptor named Rosso, now sick in the hospital.

My father went to see him, had him cared for, and when he was cured, took him to his workshop on the Boulevard Voltaire.

There he was able to cast and had every facility to use a furnace to pour his bronzes. He had him do some portraits, he executed some very nice waxes now much sought after in Italy.

He was a big man, tall, a charming friend, very Bohemian. One morning, having taken a cab to go and propose a sculpture to one of his amateurs, Eugène Marin, who, like him, lived on the Boulevard Voltaire, he [Henri] found him in the café at five, before a drink because he had not sold [the piece] and could not pay off the cab.

Rosso had married a rich Milanese[70] whose father was in the silk industry. He had had a son by her. Then he had abandoned his wife and child.

Twenty-five years later a fine young man turns up [*il voit surgir*] and says to him, "Papa, you deserted us but we are very fond of you just the same."[71] He takes him to Milan and has a house built for him.[72]

Rosso, when asked what he thought of Rodin, would answer, "Rosso loves Rosso." He maintained that Rodin had taken a great deal from him. Later there was a retrospective.[73] He was decorated.[74]

He had executed in ivory the Place de Clichy in the snow at one o'clock in the morning.[75] At the time of Carnot's murder,[76] he had hidden in the oven that had been put at his disposal because he was afraid, as an Italian, of being pursued.[77]

No friendship could have been more desirable for Rosso. Rouart's collection on the Rue de Lisbonne was open to all interested amateurs; artists and intellectuals gathered in his gracious salon. It was the perfect place in which to make contacts with the most open-minded, intellectual élite. With the introduction and backing of Henri Rouart the Paris world was open to Rosso; but although he did find clients and made some firm friends either at Rouart's or elsewhere, he remained a foreigner and an outsider, with all the frustrations that this implies.[78] In the opinion of Knud Verlow,[79] who knew him well during the first World War, he lacked the worldliness, polish, and quick wit or the extreme originality of manner and conduct that were then necessary to overcome the Parisian xenophobia. Talent was not enough. Rosso was a rough diamond, and though he managed to attract some mundane attention when he cast his bronzes at night,[80] this was not sufficient to set him afloat or to procure him important, well-paid commissions.

Henri Rouart, supposedly on the advice of Degas, commissioned Rosso to do his portrait (1889–90), thereby setting his seal of approval on the young Italian artist whom he had, so to say, discovered. The fine half-length sculpture (page 32) shows him smiling gently in the shadow of his painter's beret, his arms and hands forming a pro-

Man in the Hospital. (1889) Plaster, 9" high. The Joseph H. Hirshhorn Collection, New York

tective parenthesis to enclose his stooped body and loose smock. The muted vibration of the figure, its closely intimate quality, suggest that Rosso was more susceptible to his sitter's modesty and kindness than to the many other aspects of his rich personality.

In the early nineties, and later, Rosso failed to establish a firm connection with a dealer, who would have taken charge of his interests. He did place a work here and there when he could, at *père* Thomas or at the Galeries Georges Petit. He also entered works in official exhibitions, but for the rest, his sales to amateurs were direct, on a free-lance personal footing.[81]

Perhaps because Rosso's potential clients found his "rough" sculptures unfinished or his subjects unsuitable for their drawing rooms, he produced in close succession three works that were obviously meant to please.[82] Certainly the *Little Girl Laughing*,[83] 1890 (below), is a work that "everyone can understand." The way versions are so shiny they suggest a child's face well scrubbed. The principle of the single point of view, so obvious in the *Rouart*, is abandoned. The head stands free and can be seen from three sides. Even the back, though summarily treated, does not deny the volume of the skull. It is as though Rosso had reverted to his Milanese "types," confident that he could redeem the banal subject by making the light slither from curved surface to curved surface, halting at the cavity of the mouth. The treatment of the blind globular eyes is particularly disturbing, though beyond a doubt, given a focused tangential light, they could be made to sparkle with mischievous merriment.

Like Renoir, Rosso was pictorially attracted by the blooming complexion and smoothly rounded features of young women and children; their vulnerability, real or imagined, aroused in him deep responses of sympathy and protectiveness.

Little Girl Laughing. (1890). Wax over plaster, 10 3/4" high. Peridot Gallery, New York

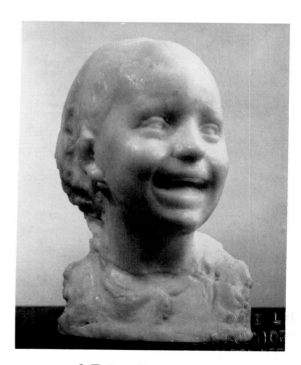

Portrait of Henri Rouart. (1890). Bronze, 40" high Galleria d'Arte Moderna, Rome

The *Petite rieuse*,[84] 1890 (page 35), is the head of a café-concert singer whose stage name was Bianca de Toledo.[85] In early versions the short-necked head emerged from somewhat suffocating garments that rose above the nape of the neck; later this environmental drapery was reduced to a frill at the right which rose to the level of the ear; in final versions the head was cut down to a mask and the line from chin to cheek was reduced and refined. The asymmetries of the features force the three-quarter view. The smiling mouth is prolonged under the right eye, more closed than the left, so that the whole face escapes and slips away from the beholder through the sinuous curves of continuous planes; no change in texture marks the eyebrows, the lashes, or the lips. Rosso must have looked at the *Mona Lisa*, though only later, in his *Yvette Guilbert*, did he capture the "enigma" of her smile.

The idea of establishing an ambiance to which the figure is bound comes to the fore again in the *Grande rieuse*,[86] 1891 (below). In the early casts

Grande rieuse. (1891). Wax over plaster, 10″ high. Galleria d'Arte Moderna, Milan

Petite rieuse. (1890). Wax over plaster, 8 3/4" high. Rosso Museum, Barzio

the bust detaches itself like a high relief from a background that is sometimes curved, sometimes trapezoidal, sometimes reduced to a concave fringe. In later versions all indications of environment disappear. The model was a healthy woman laughing freely, her teeth unconcealed by her lips; in later casts the features are less individualized, as if behind veils of aerial perspective, the eyes slurred over, the dimples at the corners of the mouth removed, the teeth less accented, but the hair is finished off in a pointed knot, and the high cheeks and the unambiguous laugh retain the blithe feeling of the artist's first idea.

An aura of courage and optimism pervades the sparkling *Child in the Sun*,[87] 1892 (page 37).

Compact, rapidly composed, the rugged baby rises out of the chalice of his swaddling clothes into the dazzling light.

In a muted mood, Rosso modeled his *Jewish Boy*,[88] 1892 (page 38), which, according to him, was a portrait of "the small Baron Rothschild."[89] On external evidence alone it is hard to believe that this was a commission, because of the forthright title and the unrelieved melancholy of the child. The modeling is rough, the hair disordered, the cheeks puffy, the chin short and pointed under the heavy lips; it might just as well be called "The Sad One." Rosso simply knew that the dejected child he had in his mind's eye was Jewish, and he named his sculpture accordingly, perhaps

Rosso in his Paris studio

Child in the Sun. (1892). Bronze, 13 1/4" high. Peridot Gallery, New York

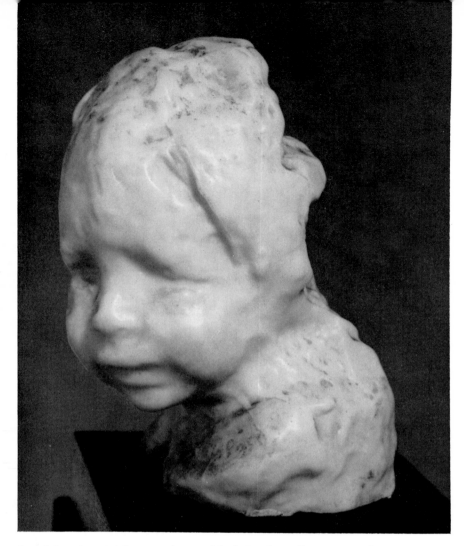

Jewish Boy. (1892). Wax over plaster, 9" high. Peridot Gallery, New York

to express his sympathy for a poor little rich boy. Rosso's turn of mind was such that he would always have been in favor of any minority or any person that aroused his sympathy, and in the Dreyfus affair he surely must have sided with Zola, his early Paris patron. In the middle nineties he executed the gay head of a woman,[90] which he exhibited with the title *Une Juive*.[91] The corners of her lips lifted in a smile, the closed left eye, and the raised right eyebrow connive to give the impression of a humorous, understanding wink. Why would he call this attractive head *Une Juive?* Only because in his own way he was shadowboxing with issues that were dividing France into two camps. He insisted on having his say and showing his colors, but he was clumsy, he used mental short cuts, he tried to compress into a title or into a set repertoire of phrases the vehemence of his beliefs. He was constantly bursting with feelings that he found hard to unravel and harder still to

put into words; in fact, his friend the painter and critic Ardengo Soffici remarked with pride that only the people who knew him well could understand what he was saying.[92]

Social indignation at the fate of the poor shows through in *Baby Chewing Bread*,[93] 1893 (page 39). The sagging, puffy cheeks, the morose eyelids, the radiating bonnet, and the envelopment of shawls from which the helpless, flattened face emerges are heart-rending in their implications. Technically it is a masterpiece of modeling and invention; the ragged wrappings wildly shredded into space bring to mind the billowing draperies of Bernini busts from which strong necks and fine heads nobly rise.

The cycle of children comes temporarily to an end with the *Sick Boy*,[94] 1893, modeled even more smoothly than the *Petite rieuse*. The head droops to the side like that of St. John in Leonardo's *Last Supper*. The eyes are closed but not

Baby Chewing Bread. (1893). Wax over plaster, 18" high. The Joseph H. Hirshhorn Collection, New York

Sick Boy. (1893). Wax over plaster, 11" high
Staatliche Skulpturensammlungen, Dresden

Sick Boy. (1893). Bronze, 10" high. Collection
Mr. and Mrs. Samuel Josefowitz, New York

slumbering, the mouth half open; a lunar pallor
emanates from the wax casts. The tight align-
ment of the minute features from domical forehead to slender chin accentuates the ovality of
the invention. In the early casts (above, left), the
back of the head is surrounded by a rippling halo
that was later removed (above, right) and substituted by vague draperies that conceal the neck
but not the beautiful line from chin to ear.[95]

Rosso's subject matter moves again to the adult
world with *Conversation in the Garden,*[96] 1893
(page 41). It represents the artist[97] seen from the
side and back, tall, heavy-shouldered, portly, and
clad from head to foot in a flowing drapery that
projects slightly at the left. He looks down at a
seated lady whose spirited movement and witty
hat make it clear that she and she alone is involved
in the conversation, while her companion listens
in silence. The sense of space is created not only
by the relation of the faceless figures placed on an
indefinite billowing platform, but by the mani-
fest play of their glances. Both the ladies look at

the artist, but he gazes only at the animated one;
the other evanesces in the vagueness of a more
distant perspective. Rosso set up the whole scene
with an extraordinary premonition of its effect
in a raking light falling from above. Whereas the
impression, one of his boldest, seems admirable
to modern eyes,[98] he did not dare exhibit it until
1905 (Kunsthaus Artaria, Vienna), perhaps because he knew intuitively that the public was not
ready for it.

The *Lady with a Veil,*[99] 1893 (page 42), is also
an impression, but on a large scale. The feminine
features are softened and merged with the brim
of the hat by a thin veil drawn tightly under the
chin, as was the fashion then. The modest jabot
ripples down from the neck, the puffed sleeves
blend with the background and the vague trim-
mings of the hat in a variety and liveliness of nu-
ances that is eminently Impressionist; the suf-
fused countenance of the passing lady can be ap-
prehended only at a second glance, pure and un-
marred by the artfully transparent wrinkles of

Conversation in the Garden. (1893). Wax over plaster,
17″ high. Collection Dr. Gianni Mattioli, Milan

BELOW: Photographed in another light

wet chiffon that distinguish the *donne velate* of Italian sculptors such as Benzoni and Spinazzi.

In November—December 1893, Rosso had occasion to show some of his sculptures in two installments at the Bodinière,[100] a hall on the Rue St.-Lazare that had been converted into an experimental theater by Charles Bodinier.[101] Because of its informal atmosphere, it soon became a favorite gathering place for the intellectual élite; conversation blossomed, everyone felt free to chat without introductions. Artists liked to show their works in the foyer, since they were sure of an intelligent and receptive audience that would carry word of their name and achievements through the salons of Paris. It is here that, in a spirit of mutual esteem and camaraderie, Rodin and Rosso exchanged works. Rodin gave Rosso a half life-size torso in bronze and took in exchange the *Petite rieuse*.[102]

Shortly afterward, Rodin must have called on Rosso in his studio, because on January 17, 1894, he sent him this short note:

My dear Rosso,

You have given me immense pleasure. Upon arriving in your studio I was struck by a wild admiration for you. I did not write you because I no longer knew your address. I am happy and if you want to lunch with me Saturday, I would be delighted.

See you soon, your friend
Rodin[103]

From a man of Rodin's proud and reserved temperament the words *folle admiration* and the elliptical *je suis heureux* are homage indeed.[104] Whether the two sculptors met for lunch, whether they saw each other often or rarely between 1894 and 1898, is uncertain.[105]

Perhaps encouraged by Rodin's interest, Rosso, in 1894, continued to work with a will and decid-

ed to explore further his idea that the figure adheres ineluctably to its cast shadow. This sensation had been etched on his retina in his student days when from the top floor of the Brera Palace he happened to see two figures crossing the courtyard in the slanting sun; the shadows they cast were so tangible that he felt he could pick them up with his hands. He was later to remark: "It happened in Milan—I didn't have to go to Paris to learn that!" In the *Bookmaker*,[106] 1894 (page 44), by tilting the figure to the left, by extending and raising the billowing ground behind it, he obtained the check-mark effect that a figure forms with its own shadow. This is an impression of Henri Rouart's son-in-law Eugène Marin[107] dressed for the races in *chapeau haut-de-forme* and redingote, leaning elegantly on his cane and holding his binoculars to his chest. The features are blurred so that only the nose is discernible, yet the whole statuette is lively and full of *allure*. Its deceptive title has led Italian critics to believe that the figure is an indictment of those who grow fat at the expense of the gullible.

In the *Man Reading*[108] (page 45), Rosso forces his experiment one step further by capturing the image from an even higher viewpoint. Looking out the window, he saw a man reading his newspaper as he strolled down the sunny street. Accordingly, he built a small figure in profile and then pushed it sharply backward against the ground, establishing a homogeneous mass, which, though it carries through to its ultimate conclusion the Impressionist principle of the assimilation of light and shadow between the figure and its environment, results in a work as hermetic as the middle stage of Cubism. Modeled in squiggles, at first glance it confuses the eye; however, when viewed from above with an overhead light, the figure stands bolt upright, magically detaching itself from the background to which it adheres. Like Brancusi, Rosso insisted that his sculpture be re-

Lady with a Veil. (1893). Wax over plaster, 27″ high
Galleria d'Arte Moderna, Rome

Bookmaker. (1894). Wax over plaster, 17 1/2" high. The Museum of Modern Art, New York
(Acquired through the Lillie P. Bliss Bequest)

Man Reading. (1894). Bronze (posthumous cast), 10″ high.
The Museum of Modern Art, New York (Harry J. Rudick Fund)

produced only from photographs taken by himself because he felt that his impressions should be seen in one light and at one angle, just as he had beheld them in their transitory reality.

In the *Yvette Guilbert*, 1894 (page 47), the experiment is reversed, because Rosso stared up at her across the glare of the footlights as he sat somewhat to the right in the darkened hall. Then twenty-five and still at the beginning of her career, Yvette Guilbert was singing at the Concert Parisien and at the Divan Japonais, but Charles Bodinier, realizing that many of his more staid habitués did not set foot in the popular café concerts, invited her to appear at matinées in his experimental Théâtre d'Application. Introduced by an earnest lecturer, she toned down her repertoire and was enthusiastically accepted as an artist, not as a ribald entertainer.[109] So charmed was she by her reception in this hall that she nicknamed it La Bodinière. Rosso probably first saw her in its sympathetic atmosphere, so that the connotations of decay and perversity that Italian critics later attached to his portrait must stem from their assumption that, as in the *Flesh of Others* and the *Bookmaker*, he was inveighing against vice.[110] Nothing could have been further from Rosso's mind when he created this sensitive animated head with thin lips unparted and nose rendered gently, when it could so easily have been caricatured in the manner of Toulouse-Lautrec. As in the *Petite rieuse*, he handled the two sides of the face quite differently, this time flattening it as in the *Child in the Sun*, and handling it with a corruscation that splinters the light. On the left, the line rises in a double curve, first concave then wavily convex, from chin to puffed hair with the barest adumbration of the eye—for this side is away from him and is blanked out by the gaslight.[111] From the right, the whole pose of the head, inclined sideways toward the audience, is borne out by the elusive shadow under the eyelid, which is accented by the high cheekbone and the lean cavity beneath it. The long and slender neck, for which Yvette Guilbert was renowned, is slashed at the right to mark the place of the famous red ribbon, and is purposely extended rather than thickened toward the back, both to blend in the light and to produce the straight line, dear to Rosso, from collarbone to hair.

Etha Fles, Rosso's later apologist and an admirer of Franz Marc and Kandinsky, was to say that he passed from Impressionism to Expressionism. This transition began with the *Conversation in the Garden*, but is even more apparent in the *Yvette Guilbert* thanks to its grand scale. Because we know her face so well we can see the many licenses Rosso took as he distilled it into a dematerialized expression of sharp wit tempered by a yielding acceptance of human frailty. The lips smile elusively but the grave eyes have the philosophical glance of the Mona Lisa.

In 1895 he composed the extraordinary *Impression on the Boulevard at Night*[112] (page 48), a work known to us only from poor photographs. Three indistinct figures are seen from the rear. The lady closest to the beholder hastens alone down the street, head bent forward, mantle billowing, as her train spreads on the pavement. Beyond her, a man supports a bonneted woman by slipping his arm around her waist from the back; they are either attempting a dance step, as one of the Italian titles suggests, or walking at a slower pace than the lady in the foreground. A photograph of the plaster cast taken close to two ladders proves that the figures were approximately life-size.[113] The sculpture, owned or stored by Mme Noblet in her country house at Jessains (Aube) near Troyes, was shattered by German gunfire in the first World War.[114]

The shift toward a larger scale, so noticeable in *Impression on the Boulevard*, is carried through in the head of *Madame X*, Rosso's most abstract work (pages 50–51). The view from the right, obligatory in the *Yvette Guilbert*, is imposed again, though the main accent is on the nose, which forms a continuous line with the compressed forehead and hair. Her left eye, a crumple of wax, is separated from the nose by a disquieting, aged, tortuous ridge that runs from the eyebrow to the lowest edge of the eye socket, her right eyebrow is raised high into the zone of the forehead, harboring the invisible eye in a pool of shadow. The mouth is minute, hardly indicated, close under the nose, the chin small and receding.

Yvette Guilbert. (1894). Terra cotta (?), 16 1/4" high. Museo d'Arte Moderna, Venice

48

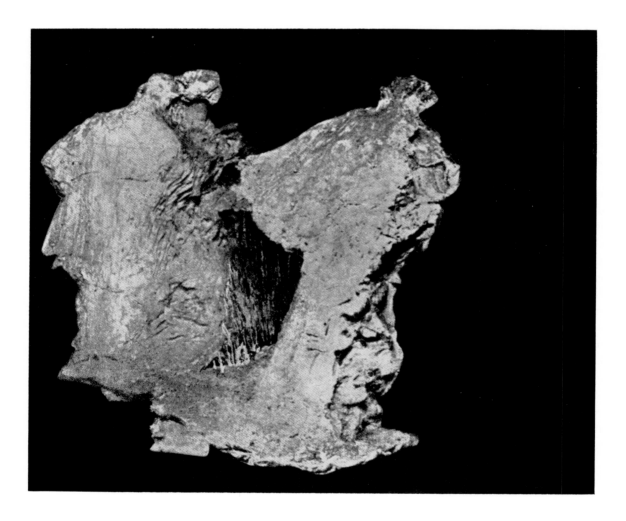

Impression on the Boulevard at Night. (1895). Plaster, probably life size. Destroyed

Etha Fles, Rosso's Dutch patroness, who knew his work as few others did, is alone in speaking of this head as the "Mask of Dolores,"[115] which she interpreted as a *persona tragica* because in it the marks of suffering, intense yet disciplined, achieve an impersonal, classical aloofness. No sculptor at this time had reached such a degree of abstraction.

Rosso's works are hard to date with precision, but none presents so wide a degree of discrepancy in point of time as the *Madame X*. Rosso's son must have been convinced that his father had worked on *Madame X* in 1913,[116] whereas in the catalogue of the 1914 Biennale, it is dated 1896.[117] Did Rosso check the dates in the catalogue? It is unlikely, for the *Ecce puer* (frontispiece and page 57) is incorrectly dated 1901.[118] Far more authoritative is the opinion of Nino Barbantini, who was then Director of the Galleria d'Arte Moderna in Venice and a close friend of Rosso and Etha Fles, from whom the Galleria received *Madame X* as a gift in the autumn of 1914. In the accession files of the museum and on the exhibition label the date is 1896. Furthermore, while Etha Fles is casual about dates, she insists in all her writings that the *Ecce puer* was Rosso's last work; had he done something new and daring thereafter, she would have been the first to hail it.[119] A possible solution for the problem is provided by the remark of Christian Zervos who said of *Madame X*, "But it was only a sketch!"[120] And, indeed, it may have remained at the plaster stage in Rosso's studio for years.[121] But as time went by, what with the encouragement of Etha Fles, who had a sincere admiration for German Expressionism, and his own friendship for Modigliani,[122] he may have come to see this "sketch" in a twentieth-century light and decided to finish it in wax to swell his entries in the Biennale.[123] By 1913 he had long since made contact with his son who might, when he was preparing his father's monograph with Mino Borghi just before 1950, have insisted on the date 1913 either because he remembered seeing his father working on the head, possibly in Milan, or because he wanted to prove that the latter had been "creative" until 1913.[124]

It would be interesting to know the circumstances of Rosso's next undertaking, the portrait of Madame Noblet of 1897 (page 52). The sitter's husband, Dr. Noblet, was Rosso's physician as well as a personal friend. Rosso often visited them at their villa in Jessains near Troyes.[125] Did he embark on the portrait to pay his medical bills, or was he actually asked to do it and suitably remunerated? Irrelevant though this question may seem, all that relates to Rosso's physical and mental health is worth exploring in connection with the desultoriness, and final halt, of his productivity. Commissioned or not, this was the first portrait of a patron and close friend that he had undertaken since the *Henri Rouart* of 1890. Undaunted by the consideration that if Mme Noblet troubled to pose, she might want a charming and even ornamental image of herself, he roughed out a large ponderous bust to be seen, as usual, from the beholder's right. Her left eye, nose, and mouth carry the message of resemblance, while the other side of her face is rubbed out except for a slight indication of eyebrow and eye socket, beyond which four cursory indentations of Rosso's fingers in the clay create the rippling shadow from hair to shoulder which gives relief to the three-quarter view. The neckless head is embedded in a tight-fitting blouse, while tremendous bulges at the left suggest the gathered puffs of fashionable sleeves. And yet, with all this willful awkwardness, the portrait has an extraordinary quality of intimacy and warmth.

Madame X. (1896). Wax, 12″ high. Museo d'Arte Moderna, Venice

Madame X (side view)

SUSPENDED ACTIVITY, 1897—1900

Looking back from 1897—always provided that the generally accepted dates are reliable—we observe that Rosso's last fruitful year was 1894. In each subsequent year he produced one single work: in 1895, *Impression on the Boulevard at Night;* in 1896, *Madame X;* and in 1897, *Madame Noblet.* Already in 1894, at thirty-six, when he did the *Conversation in the Garden,* he knew himself to be as corpulent as a middle-aged man. It is hard to fathom whether the many periods of half-starvation he had gone through caused him to overeat, or whether the illness at the Lariboisière Hospital was a premonitory signal of disorders that were to become chronic. A survey of the events of the late nineties may prove indirectly enlightening.

In 1896, he went to London because some of his works were exhibited in a Pre-Raphaelite show at Boussod and Valadon.[126]

In 1897 a certain preliminary excitement over Rodin's *Balzac* (right) was already in the air; it was shown in plaster, half life-size, at the Salon de la Nationale in 1898,[127] where it was a *succès de scandale* and brought its author considerable notoriety. The minute Rosso laid eyes on it he was convinced that Rodin had "taken a great deal from him." But what had Rodin taken? Rosso and his defender Etha Fles maintained that precisely the *Man in the Hospital* (page 31; seen by Rodin at the Bodinière late in 1893) had influenced the *Balzac;* unfortunately neither of them was ever to specify whether the impressionist modeling, the strongly emotional overtones, the connection between the figure and the ground, or the shrouding hospital dressing gown motivated their belief. In 1894, when Rodin presented a plaster sketch of the projected monument to his patrons, the Société des Gens de Lettres, his *Balzac* was still nude, with strong arms crossed above a resilient stomach.[128] Rosso's *Man in the Hospital* may have had a gradual, even subcon-

scious effect on the course of Rodin's tireless and thoughtful experimentation; it would not be reasonable to brush aside the opinions of Rosso and Etha Fles, because theirs is the closest evidence in point of time. But in Rosso's studio at the end of 1893, Rodin would also have observed the *Conversation in the Garden* (page 41), and if he con-

Auguste Rodin. *Monument to Balzac.* (1897). Bronze (posthumous cast, 1954), 9' 3" high. The Museum of Modern Art, New York (Presented in memory of Curt Valentin by his friends)

OPPOSITE: *Madame Noblet.* (1897). Bronze, 26 1/2" high Galleria d'Arte Moderna, Milan

tinued to keep an eye on the Italian sculptor for whom he had such a "wild admiration," he would have seen the *Bookmaker* (page 44) and the *Man Reading* (page 45), both of 1894.[129] In these three pieces, the figures, like tree trunks, sprout from the ground at surprising angles, and it is precisely the slant of the Rodin *Balzac,* a slant sideways and backward, that strikes dispassionate observers as Rodin's heaviest debt to Rosso (pages 72–73). The same device of shadow-casting that makes the male figure in the *Conversation* so ominous in his downward look and Eugène Marin of the *Bookmaker* so stylish in his sideways stance is used by Rodin to give the *Balzac,* defiantly slanted backward, its expression of proud grandeur. In fact, the figure is so perilously tilted that the base behind the half-concealed feet is prolonged to prevent it from toppling.

What sort of acknowledgment, public or private, could Rosso have expected for such an intangible debt? Quite apart from the fact that Rodin was notoriously ungenerous, surely Rosso cannot have expected him to write a note of acknowledgment or pay a deferential call to declare his gratitude. Only an exceptionally magnanimous artist, then or now, would dream of admitting an artistic obligation toward someone younger and less famous than himself.[130]

In the spring of 1898, two critics raised their voices in Rosso's defense, Camille de Sainte-Croix and Yveling Rambaud; but the authoritative Charles Morice, who had written enthusiastic pieces about him in 1895, 1896, and 1897, remained prudently silent. Rosso himself at this time was probably in one of his morose and vulnerable moods. Had he been deeply involved in new works, he might have been furious, but he would not have taken the matter so much to heart. Alas, the wound cut deep. In 1905, in Vienna, he spoke often and resentfully about Rodin to Mrs. Ida Maria Sachs;[131] during the war he harped on the same subject with Knud Verlow; and after the war, with Ardengo Soffici and with his new Venetian friend Mario Vianello Chiodo. Between 1904 and 1910, he repeatedly exhibited for comparison with his own sculptures the torso Rodin had given him as well as photographs of the *Balzac* and of the *Despair.*

That Rosso did not take this reverse in stride is a revelatory symptom of his state of mind in the late nineties. Since 1894 he had slowed down, and the capacity to create came to him sporadically. He had no dealer, no encouragement; it is reasonable to surmise that to make ready money he recast old works, which he marketed himself. From the artless record of his son's reminiscences, one senses that he frequented the Rouarts, that he met Degas at least once,[132] that he ran into Toulouse-Lautrec,[133] that he dropped by *père* Tanguy's shop at 14, Rue Clausel.[134] For the rest, his daily life is shrouded in mystery. Did he see his two countrymen Boldini and Zandomeneghi? Did he attempt to make a connection with Carrière, whose art both in subject matter and in the sacrifice of color in favor of luministic effects had such affinities with his own? Did he attempt to ally himself with the Symbolists, with whom idealistically he would have had much in common?[135] While it is possible that in his later years in Milan he mentioned other names that we would recognize but his son forgot, it is even more probable that he lived a solitary and moody life.[136]

LAST WORKS. PURSUIT OF FAME

In 1900, the Commissioners for the loans of Italian art to the Exposition Universelle saw fit to discard Rosso. This affront, coming as it did less than two years after his vexation with Rodin, marks a turning point in Rosso's attitude. He became belligerent. From 1900 to 1914, and in a lesser way till his death in 1928, he fought for his art *unguibus et rostris*. Had he not become so intent on asserting himself, he might have been more open to new inspirations and more willing to submit himself to the torture of creation.[137] However, for an artist of Rosso's temperament, where all depended on the warmth of emotion, new works could not come to fruition in a mood of defensiveness and indignation.

At the last moment and too late for the catalogue of the Exposition, Rosso's old Milanese friend, the dealer Alberto Grubicy, arranged to have five of his sculptures exhibited near the paintings of the celebrated Giovanni Segantini.[138] Arsène Alexandre wrote his first piece on Rosso for *Figaro,* and Louis Vauxcelles (who was later the first to use in print the terms Fauves and Cubism) reported on him in *Gil Blas.*

Vittore Grubicy, Alberto's brother, had lived in Holland in the nineties and had many friends among the members of the Dutch Society of Etchers, so probably through this chain of acquaintances Rosso was introduced to one of the Dutch Commissioners to the Exposition, Miss Etha Fles, herself a painter and etcher. Full of vitality, a dauntless idealist, she was at forty-three as excitable as a young girl. In this "giant with the soul of a boy" she perceived instantly the incarnation of the natural man unspoiled by society, who could pour into his art all that was purest and most transcendental in the human spirit. With her, action followed impulse, and while still in Paris she organized for Holland a circulating exhibition of Impressionists in which Rosso would be starred as the unique sculptor worthy of such a classification. In addition, she commissioned him to do a portrait of her father, a highly respected oculist.

We next find Rosso in Utrecht, feverishly modeling the full-length image of the old doctor seated in the garden of the Fles mansion on the Maliebaan. Why ever did Rosso attempt the entire life-size figure in modern jacket and trousers? Why did he not restrict himself to a bust like the splendid *Henri Rouart*?[139] Original photographs of the portrait are unavailable; one of its several reproductions shows the plaster figure installed close to a sofa which provides a clue to its scale. The clearest illustration[140] reveals the grave face of an old man with curly tufts of hair and a flowing mustache; the rest of the slumping figure is quite unrealized. A head by Jan Veth, executed in 1895,[141] proves that Rosso had caught the resemblance and instilled it with the pathos and resignation of advancing age.[142]

While Rosso was intermittently busy with the portrait, the Impressionist exhibition was displayed in Amsterdam, Utrecht, The Hague, and Rotterdam. Miss Fles supervised its publicity and drew all possible attention to the great Italian sculptor. After a stay in Holland, Rosso proceeded to Germany where he had exhibitions in Berlin, Krefeld, Leipzig, and Dresden.[143]

By 1902, Rosso's name was no longer obscure. Julius Meier-Graefe called at his studio and took notes, which he later published, providing "good quotes"[144] for Rosso's propaganda, but at the same time not declaring himself openly in favor of either Rosso or Rodin in the controversy that, by then, had reached a certain degree of asperity. It is probably thanks to Meier-Graefe that the Italian sculptor was invited to participate in the annual exhibition of the Vienna Secession of 1903, which had as its theme Impressionism in painting and sculpture. The exhibition was to open January 17, 1903. Accordingly, Rosso, the restless traveler, set off on the train. But somehow, just before reaching Vienna, he met with an accident or became violently ill. He was carried unconscious to the Sophienspital near the Westbahnhof, where he remained for several days.[145] In later years he was to tell his friends that a fall in Vienna had impaired his creative faculties.[146] Eventually recovered, he settled in the Hôtel de France in Vienna for a long stay. The collectors Hermann and Gottfried Eissler were much taken with him, and after considerable bargaining they acquired his "beautiful casts" of a *Roman Senator*[147] and a *Julius Caesar*. Rosso's Italian friends speak favorably of his copies from the antique, but the fact that he was willing to sell them proves that although he detested classical and Renaissance art, he had such pride in his skill as a craftsman and caster that he considered his copies not as exercises but as new creations on which he had set his personal imprint.

Rosso remained in Vienna until summer when, by devious stages, he started off for Paris. In Brussels he fell ill again and wrote of himself as an "old crate, but still solid," a strange remark for a man of forty-five. This relapse was frustrating since he was eager to get back to Paris to prepare for a "big exhibition"; apparently in the summer of 1903 he already knew that he was slated to show in the Salon d'Automne of 1904 as one of its charter members.[148] Because he considered himself still unappreciated in France, he was anxious to put his best foot forward and, indeed, when the time came, he was able to present some twenty pieces.[149]

Although he was refused a gallery to himself, he had some say in the placing of his entries. He selected rooms adjacent to the exhibits of his former friend Troubetzkoy, whom he now considered a rival, so that the public could compare their relative merits.[150] Two installation photographs survive: one shows his *Baby Chewing Bread* near a Cézanne *Bathers* then owned by Auguste Pellerin; the other reveals an elaborate enthronement of the *Man in the Hospital* that only Rosso himself could have devised. On the wall he hung three large photographs: an enlargement of the old woman from his *Impression in an Omnibus*, Rodin's *Balzac* cut below the waist,[151] and a cast of a large male head (not the Dresden *Vitellius*); in front of these photographs, on a table, the *Man in the Hospital,* and beside it, his small copy of Michelangelo's Medici *Madonna*.[152] The notices of Louis Vauxcelles and Stéphane Cloud[153]

as well of those of correspondents to foreign papers must have pleased Rosso, but he could not have foreseen at the time that Ardengo Soffici's report in *L'Europe artiste* would be the most significant of all for the propagation of his fame in his own country.

However, money more than praise was important at this time. Rosso kept hoping to make a profitable sale to a museum, but in the late months of 1904, still crippled by the expenses he had incurred for his show at the Salon d'Automne, he was impelled to ask his Austrian friend Harald Gutherz[154] for a loan, which he promised to repay in Vienna within a few months.

Ever since the Secession exhibition of 1903, the Kunsthaus Artaria, once Beethoven's publishers, had been transacting with Rosso for a one-man show. After elaborate preparations supervised by the ever-demanding sculptor,[155] and accompanied by an elaborate booklet in which Rosso's past favorable critiques were quoted at length, the exhibition opened on February 10, 1905, with no less than seventeen sculptures, photographs of two figures from the *Impression in an Omnibus*, a photograph of the portrait of Dr. Fles, and—as comparison pieces—the Rodin torso and seven of Rosso's copies of sculptures of past periods.[156]

Ludwig Hevesy was the first critic to realize that here, indeed, was a major figure who deserved a careful study; his article in *Kunst und Kunsthandwerk* (1905) is the first serious analysis of Rosso's work and of his liberating role in contemporary sculpture. Justifiably elated by his reception, Rosso nevertheless was overcome by loneliness; unable to speak German, he clung for warmth to his few Viennese friends who knew French or Italian. Mrs. Ida Maria Sachs, then Mrs. Brünhof, remembers him in revelatory ways. Every day he would send her a note by hand or a telegram with greetings, some flowers perhaps, or the suggestion of a meeting later in the day. When he realized that she couldn't decide what to call her infant daughter, he enjoined, "Call her something fine, something healthy, call her 'Beefsteak.' " Already at this time he hated to walk because his feet were small, his shoes tight, and his weight great. Between the lunch and dinner

Ecce puer. (1906—7). Wax, 17″ high. Collection Mr. and Mrs. Harry L. Winston, Birmingham, Michigan

hour he used to induce the Italian headwaiter of his favorite restaurant to go for a drive with him in a cab. One day, in great agitation he informed Mrs. Brünhof that a member of the Lanckoroński family had visited his exhibition but had not bought. He forced her to go with him in a carriage to the Lanckoroński palace; he rang the bell, was received by a butler, and kept waiting in a grand front hall. Quickly he fetched several bundles from the carriage, removed the Roman heads from their pedestals, and substituted his own work. When the master of the house appeared, Rosso exclaimed, "Look how much more lively my sculptures are than this garbage!" But the irate Lanckoroński did not buy.[157]

In these years Rosso ran where fortune called. In his tour of conquest we find him next in London for an exhibition of the International Society (February—March 1906) and for a one-man show at the Eugene Cremetti Gallery (1906—7), for which a glorious album was printed at the expense of Etha Fles.[158]

Thanks to these exhibitions Rosso received the commission to do the portrait of Alfred William Mond, then five or six years old (frontispiece;

page 57). The child was the son of Emile Mond, nephew of Dr. Ludwig Mond whose renowned collection was to pass to the National Gallery in 1910.[159] Possibly Rosso had executed some heads since the unappreciated portrait of Dr. Fles but none are definitely recorded.[160]

He embarked on the new assignment with apprehension; in fact, the drama of what was to be his last creation has not only been recounted many times in print, but remained alive in the minds of those who, like Signora Tilde Rosso, his daughter-in-law, knew and loved him. She told the story as though it had happened the day before.[161] There he was, a guest in a wealthy home because he was supposed to do the portrait of the little boy. He saw the child daily in the natural course of living with the family. Try as he might, he couldn't produce a thing. He was overstaying his welcome, he was beside himself. One evening there was a reception, the drawing room was full of elegant guests. Suddenly a curtain was drawn aside a few inches, the little boy peered in, his lips parted in amazement, and he was gone. Triggered by this snapshot vision, Rosso rushed to his room, worked through the night

Rosso in Etha Fles's apartment, about 1908

and into the next day until he had brought the head to completion. He was found asleep on a couch still dressed in his evening clothes. It is said that the family did not consider the portrait a good likeness, but Rosso kept the model and in later years cast it many times in wax-covered plaster, and perhaps in bronze. He called it *Ecce puer*—Behold the child—and said of it, "Voilà la vision de pureté dans un monde banal."

The dainty features, modeled with extreme delicacy, are foiled by the rasped vertical incisions at the right which veil part of the temple and neck, as the half-open curtain had once done. The lips breathe, the vivid eyes glance, the blond hair surges above the tall shiny brow through an uncanny transmission of life. If for 1907 (the year

of Picasso's *Demoiselles d'Avignon*) we consider increased abstraction the chief measure of progress, then the *Ecce puer* represents a retrogression over Rosso's sculptures of the mid-nineties, all of which contain more daring distortions and a conscious departure from reality. But as a statement, this work is the distillation of Rosso's compassion, tenderness, and nostalgia for men's first innocent years. Through it he looked back at his own childhood while, figuratively, he caressed and exalted all children.[162]

Back from England, in 1907 Rosso had the satisfaction of being bought by the State (*acheté par l'Etat*): thanks to the mediation of Georges Clemenceau, the *Ecce puer* and the *Lady with a Veil* entered the Luxembourg.[163]

RECOGNITION IN ITALY

In Florence at this time Ardengo Soffici,[164] with Giuseppe Prezzolini and Giovanni Papini, was planning a new periodical, *La Voce*, which for four years was to blow a gust of fresh air into the lethargic and insular atmosphere of bourgeois Italy. It was deeply and controversially involved in politics, sociology, and literature, as well as the arts; in fact, to this day its yellowed numbers make fascinating reading. The most disparate subjects were discussed with a directness, an enlightened vision, and a contempt for accepted conventions that are still startlingly fresh.

The first number of *La Voce* (December 1908) carried an advance book review of Soffici's *Il caso Medardo Rosso*, which was to appear in March 1909. It was the first shot in the campaign to launch the self-exiled sculptor in his own country. All through 1909 article followed article extolling his art, so admired in the rest of Europe, so shamefully ignored in Italy. Not content with

words, and feeling that evidence should be shown, Soffici and Prezzolini laid plans for a grand exhibition in which their protégé would appear in the worthiest company they could devise. Unlike most of their countrymen at that time, they were well traveled, and in Paris, their artistic Mecca, they felt familiar and certain of their judgment.

They set their sights high and thus were faced with the difficulty of raising money to cover the costs of the show. For backing or for loans of pictures they approached Bernard Berenson, Leo Stein, Carlo Loeser, Egisto Fabbri, Carlo Placci—all well-known personalities associated with the Florence of that period. The collector Gustavo Sforni seems in the end to have made up the financial deficit.[165] The exhibition, entitled *Prima Mostra dell'Impressionismo e di Medardo Rosso*, opened on April 20, 1910, in the gloomy rooms of the Florentine Lyceum, at 28, Via Ricasoli. Loans arrived from Paul Rosenberg, Durand-

Ruel, and Vollard, as well as from private collectors, and Rosso himself sailed in with some sixteen or eighteen pieces, and his Rodin torso, to make his first appearance in Italy in the company of Degas, Monet, Renoir, Cézanne, Pissarro, Toulouse-Lautrec, van Gogh, Picasso, Sisley, Matisse, and Forain.[166]

Rosso firmly believed in establishing an equation between himself and other artists. He told his son that he had exhibited *with* Carrière, *with* Lautrec, *with* Burne-Jones, implying that he was as good as they were; in 1904, he wrote Gutherz that his sculptures in the Salon d'Automne were installed close to Cézannes and Renoirs and that they looked well with them, "proving" that he was "right." He exhibited versions of past sculptures as comparison pieces with his own; he showed the Rodin torso at the Artaria and in the Lyceum, and may well have suggested the general lines of the Florence exhibition to Soffici and Prezzolini. His passion for self-assertion by association was such that while in Florence he even managed to set up one of his pieces in the Accademia beside one of Michelangelo's Captives.[167]

But after 1910, as if, at last, he understood that he could stand on his own feet, he never resorted to comparisons again. He still liked to have his pieces exhibited close to paintings and not isolated in bare galleries, because his highly sensitive eyes saw color reflections in his sculptures and he felt that in the vicinity of pictures they were chromatically more alive. In 1911, when invited to show at the Esposizione Internazionale di Belle Arti in Rome, he was annoyed with the commissioners because of delays and installation disagreements. In 1914, when at long last he was invited to show at the Venice Biennale, he characteristically arrived late, leaning on the arm of his son. Because he had neglected to answer the official invitation to exhibit, the galleries that had been reserved for him were hung with Mancini's paintings, but he was willing to install his twenty sculptures in the same space; they received color from the pictures, and that was all that mattered to him.

While his entries in Rome had not gone unnoticed, his large one-man show in Venice was applauded by foreign and Italian critics, and most especially by Nino Barbantini who wrote six pieces about him in 1914, not only because of the exhibition itself but because the Venice Galleria d'Arte Moderna was about to receive important gifts of Rosso's works.

In March 1913, Rosso's dedicated patroness Etha Fles, who had been living in Rome since 1908, decided to move from Italy, and hit upon the idea of donating her collection to Italian museums, with the provision that each recipient should purchase one sculpture directly from the artist. She had first opened transactions with the Museo Civico of Turin where, because of dissensions within the board, some gifts of hers were accepted though nothing was bought from Rosso in return. She was more successful in Rome, where she induced the Galleria d'Arte Moderna to acquire the *Lady with a Veil* in return for three gifts from her collection. In Venice, thanks to Barbantini's true interest in Rosso, arrangements were much easier, so much so that not only she, but Rosso himself, donated works to the Galleria d'Arte Moderna in the Ca' Pesaro. When Etha Fles left Italy in 1915 there were no less than sixteen Rossos in Italian museums; without her foresight and determination probably no works by him would have entered Italian public collections before his death.

ROSSO AND THE FUTURISTS

Rosso's name would not, however, have sunk into oblivion, for the Futurists, and especially Boccioni, hailed him as a unique Italian precursor. On February 20, 1909, the front page of the Paris *Figaro* had carried Marinetti's Futurist Manifesto, which contained the exclamations, "Burn the libraries! Flood the museums!"—a furious repudiation of Italy's artistic past and its present climate of apathy and sentimentality.

Rosso, the impassioned anti-classicist, should have welcomed this cry of rebellion which echoed his own protesting attitude of the past thirty years. He, too, had found the weight of the classics unendurable, and had attained artistic manhood only when he had managed to wipe out all

tradition and academic training. Had Marinetti launched his manifesto in the middle eighties or even in the nineties, Rosso might have joined the young Italian firebrands; but in 1909 it was too late. At fifty-one, set in his ways, egocentric, indifferent to new ideas, Rosso was repelled by the Futurist exaltation of the clangor of modern life. Were these countrymen of his completely inhuman?[168] They planned to take Paris by storm, but Rosso, a seasoned Parisian, sensed that they had every chance of going off half-cocked. When the Futurist exhibition opened at Bernheim-Jeune's on February 5, 1912, Marinetti claimed that it was an overwhelming success, but Guillaume Apollinaire's first reaction was patroniz-

Rosso shortly before World War I

62

Umberto Boccioni. *Anti-Graceful (The Artist's Mother).*
(1912). Bronze, 23" high. Collection Mr. and Mrs. Harry
L. Winston, Birmingham, Michigan

Umberto Boccioni. *Development of a Bottle in Space.*
(1912). Bronze, 15" high. The Museum of Modern Art,
New York (Aristide Maillol Fund)

ing: "As for Futurist art, it makes one smile slightly, in Paris, though it should not make Italians smile, because if it does, so much the worse for them."[169] Paris could afford to be condescending but Apollinaire, who knew his Italy,[170] felt that Futurism should create a healthy ferment there. Within a very short time he became more involved with the young Italians and wrote about them in such a way that his allegiance seemed to waver between them and the Cubists to whom he was committed.

In April 1912, when Rosso received Boccioni's *Technical Manifesto of Futurist Sculpture*, he did not respond, although it contained passages that did him flattering and discerning homage:

> Medardo Rosso [is] the only great modern sculptor who has attempted to widen the scope of sculpture by rendering plastically the effect of environment upon the subject, as well as the ties that bind it to the surrounding atmosphere. . . .

Medardo Rosso's work is revolutionary and most modern, more profound,[171] and necessarily narrower in range. Absent from it is the agitation of heroes or symbols; the plane of a woman's brow or of a child's forehead gives evidence of a liberation of space that is far more important as a record of the human spirit than has as yet been perceived. Unfortunately, the limitations of impressionism restricted Medardo Rosso's experiments to a sort of low or high relief, proving that he still conceived the human figure traditionally, as a world to itself and as an episode.

Medardo Rosso's revolution, though highly important, starts from a point of view that is purely pictorial and external; it neglects the problem of a new construction of planes; like the light impressionist brushstrokes, it gives a sense of lively immediacy, but, by requiring a rapid execution from life, it divests the work of art of its character of universality. It therefore has the same advantages and the same faults as impressionist painting; our aesthetic revolution originated from these experiments, but it continued and pursued them to their extreme opposite goal.[172]

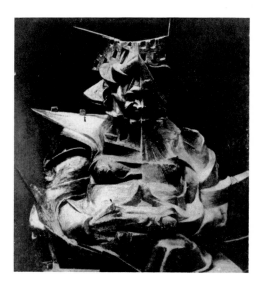

Umberto Boccioni. *Head + House + Light.* (1912)
Various materials. Destroyed

What Boccioni admired in Rosso was the impinging pressure of the environment upon the subject and the extension of the subject into its surroundings. His portrait of his mother, *Anti-Graceful* (page 62) and his *Development of a Bottle in Space* (page 62), both 1912, carry the idea of interpenetration several steps further than Rosso ever had, with a crisp handling of the shifting planes. To use Longhi's words, Rosso had "raised the surface substance of things into the most refined mud-petals and fried them in the atmospheric whirl"; his aim was to create a "halo with a sharper or softer focus of forms in the rapid transience of light."[173] Boccioni was deeply absorbed in the relationship of his masses and the projections that sprout from the half-concealed inner form. The hollows and grooves that imprison the circumambient air are sharply profiled and formal, not improvised with the thumb into nodules, fringes, and pictorial scumbles. His surfaces are finished, glossy, volumetrically interrelated, not dependent for their effect on a special light. In the portrait of his mother, in the *Concave and Convex Abstraction of a Head*, 1912,[174] in the *Head + House + Light*, 1912 (page 63), he adopts Rosso's asymmetrical handling of the human features, but not for purposes of foreshortening, nor to enforce a single point of view. What interested Boccioni was Rosso's "liberation of space"; he cared nothing for his sentiment, rendering of mood, and social commentary.

The Futurist accolade left Rosso unmoved; yet he remained loyal to his friends Soffici, Prezzolini, and Papini. Always personal rather than conceptual, he paid no attention to the complicated conflicts and rapprochements between them and the Futurists, just as he ignored the death of *La Voce* and the birth of the pro-Futurist *Lacerba*, both of which favored Italy's entry in the war on the side of France and England.

By 1915, Rosso had returned to his studio at 98, Boulevard des Batignolles. Every day he would wander to the Rue Jacob to see his Danish friend Knud Verlow or he would forgather with Amedeo Modigliani. Indifferent to the devastation of Reims Cathedral, he exclaimed Futuristically: "Destroy the monuments, we'll build better ones!" The war's senseless bloodshed shocked him deeply; had he not always advocated a *patria illimitata*—a fatherland without boundaries? He tried to convince individuals not to take part in the conflict, he even inveighed against his dearest Italian friends because they had not refused to join the armed forces and were now fighting at the front.

On November 17, 1917, Rodin died. Eight months later, when critics and admirers had finished with their eulogies, Guillaume Apollinaire wrote an extraordinary paragraph about Rosso in *L'Europe nouvelle*: "The death of Rodin did not cause art critics to speak again about Medar-do Rosso who is now, beyond a doubt, the greatest living sculptor. The injustice of which this prodigious sculptor has always been a victim is not about to be repaired. Meanwhile, Medardo Rosso works in silence in Paris. In the quiet of his studio he evokes the aspect of those Renaissance artists who were both sculptors and casters, masters and workmen at the same time, doing everything themselves. Medardo Rosso has not submitted new works to the judgment of the public for a long time. He is thinking of modeling the figure of a horse."[175]

Apollinaire, the most discerning avant-garde critic in Europe died of Spanish fever three months after writing the very words that Rodin's rival had been waiting for since 1898. Did Rosso ever see them? Did Etha Fles? Probably not because they are never quoted.[176]

Some time during the war Medardo Rosso hid his most precious belongings in a mound of clay,[177] locked his studio, and moved to Milan.[178]

THE LAST DECADE

In the tempest of the four war years Rosso imagined that all echoes of his fame were silenced. The eloquent and fervid Boccioni, his only conscious follower, had died in 1916. The whole struggle for renown had to be resumed. In October 1920, Rosso entered his *Concierge* and *Jewish Boy* in the Venice exhibition of religious art by changing their titles to, respectively, *St. Ursula* and *Child of Nazareth* or *St. Louis* (Gonzaga).[179] At this time, or shortly after, in the house of Venetian acquaintances,[180] he made new friends: Mario Vianello Chiodo, whose devotion and unflagging zeal did much to help and encourage him, and Margherita Sarfatti, who was to become Mussolini's adviser in all matters pertaining to art. From the very first she took a personal interest in Rosso, and when, after the March on Rome, she was in a position to wield her influence in Fascist circles, she always kept him in mind. In 1923, she hailed his one-man show at the Bottega di Poesia in Milan; in 1925, she praised him in her book *Segni colori e luci*; and when, in 1926, he showed in the *Prima Mostra del Novecento* in Milan[181] and was represented in an Italian exhibition at the Grand Central Galleries in New York, she wrote two more pieces about him within the same year.

Old friends had rallied, too, most notably Barbantini, Soffici, and the painter Carlo Carrà. Immediately after the war, the faithful Etha Fles wrote a long article about him for the Dutch periodical *Elsevier*; later she had a shorter one in *Cronache d'Italia*; in 1922, she put out a little book in German; and in 1928, the year of Rosso's death, she published a collection of memoirs, in which Rosso's name frequently recurs.[182]

In the perspective of time Rosso came to view his works critically. His eight favorites were *Ecce puer, Man in the Hospital, Man Reading, Baby Chewing Bread, Jewish Boy, Madame Noblet, Lady with a Veil,* and the portrait of Henri Rouart. Upon hearing this, Carrà remonstrated, "But what about the two *rieuses* and the *Flesh of Others*?" Rosso answered, "Those are still objective expressions, and they contain less of the spatial, dominantly contrasting, tonality. They transmit less clearly than the others the emotion and the unification of light, space, and air."[183]

Puzzling though these remarks may seem, they are lucid in comparison with Rosso's statements published in the twenties and his many extant letters from 1906 to his death. His friends prided themselves in understanding him and were, in fact, charmed by his conversation, which was always cordial, forceful, repetitious, and a bit incoherent. He sent streams of telegrams and wrote atrociously illegible letters scattered with single words in huge minuscules centered on the page,[184] inscrutable allusions, indictments, proclamations in mixed languages, multiple postscripts, re-salutations, and embraces which rival in free association, though not in poetic content, the writings of Gertrude Stein and James Joyce. And though Soffici and Prezzolini are convinced that his way of writing and speaking had no direct influence on the *parole in libertà* of the Futurists, they delighted in Rosso's glorious demolition of grammar, syntax, and linguistic consistency.

Since his Lyceum show in 1910, Rosso had established himself among his Italian friends not only as an admirable artist but also as an eccentric. He basked in the warmth of their indulgent and sincere affection, and he would travel to Rome, Florence, and Venice to see them. As diabetes made its inroads, he came to depend more on the companionship of his Milanese friends Carlo Carrà and his charming wife, and on the composer Umberto Giordano.[185] For help and comfort he relied on his son and daughter-in-law, who loved him dearly. Increasingly confined to his room, he still insisted, like so many invalids, on doing things himself instead of calling for assistance; one day, struggling with a heavy dresser, he wounded his foot; eventually gangrene set in. Before consenting to an amputation, he asked his surgeon to guarantee that the operation would be successful, so that he could really count on going back to his dear Paris. He was emphatically reassured. His last recorded words bear witness to the anxiety and unremitting self-doubt that besets all true artists in the first moments of creation. "These doctors," he exclaimed, "they are always so certain! I never felt certain when I started a new work"[186]

Notes to the Text

[1] Biographers agree that before his army service he painted, but none of these early works has as yet been identified. He seemingly received no formal training until he entered the Brera Academy in 1882, at the age of twenty-four; nevertheless, his portrait of Baldassare Surdi, of 1883 (p. 17), and his large drawing of his dead mother, of 1884 (p. 21), reveal a knowledgeable assurance that he could scarcely have acquired in less than a year at the Academy.

[2] One of these was Count Besozzi of Turin to whom Rosso gave a bronze of his *Mother and Child Sleeping* (now in the collection of Sig. Cesare Fasola, Bagno a Ripoli, Florence). Another was Gastone Pesce who was later, from 1895 to 1911, technical consultant to the Italian Embassy in Paris. It is not unreasonable to surmise that Pesce is the "engineer friend" who in 1883 asked Rosso to send sculptures to Paris at the request of galleries (Mino Borghi, *Medardo Rosso*, Milan, Il Milione, 1950, p. 21), and that it was upon his encouragement that Rosso ventured to the French capital in 1884. Also, during Rosso's absence from Paris 1884—89, either Pesce or, if not he, then

Vittore Grubicy (see note 9), saw to it that his sculptures were exhibited as often and as worthily as possible. (See also, note 50.)

[3] Etha Fles, *Medardo Rosso*, Freiburg (Baden), Walter Heinrich, 1922, p. 9.

[4] Their use of color is not in any way reflected in Rosso's portrait of Baldassare Surdi.

[5] For a more detailed discussion of early influences on Rosso and the artistic atmosphere in Milan, see Luciano Caramel, "La prima attività di Medardo Rosso e i suoi rapporti con l'ambiente milanese," *Arte Lombarda*, VI, 2, December 1961. See also Enrico Somarè, "La Scultura di Medardo Rosso," *L'Esame* (Milan), VI, 1, March 1939.

[6] A Congress on the Unity of the Arts was held in Amsterdam in the winter of 1862—63.

[7] Louis Piérard, *Un sculpteur impressioniste: Medardo Rosso*, Paris, Editions de la Société Nouvelle, 1909, p. 4.

[8] Charles Baudelaire, *The Mirror of Art*, tr. and ed. Jonathan Mayne, Garden City, New York, Doubleday Anchor Books, 1956, pp. 119ff.

[9] Born in Milan, of a Hungarian father and Italian mother. Such was his enthusiasm for Jongkind, and the French Impressionists, that at thirty-two, with no previous training, he began to etch and paint. He produced delicate "divisionist" landscapes and wrote a great deal to publicize Impressionism while maintaining a separate enthusiasm for the Lombard school. He and, later, his brother Alberto were Segantini's dealers.

[10] Emilio Lavagnino, *L'arte moderna dai neoclassici ai contemporanei*, Turin, UTET, 1961, pp. 1124ff.

[11] *El locch, El lucc, Il vagabondo, A zonzo.*

[12] For the chronology of Rosso's early works I follow roughly the sequence established by Caramel (*op. cit.*), and for the later work, that of Borghi (*op. cit.*). I believe, however, that Rosso worked on several pieces at once, so that an exact chronology cannot be achieved.

[13] The untranslatable Italian word *macchietta* expresses the combination of a character study often bordering on caricature and a specific indication of social class or profession derived both from the French tradition of *arts-et-métiers* prints and from the increasingly individualized Neapolitan carved figures for crèches (*presepi*).

[14] *El cantant a spass, Cantante senza scrittura, Le chanteur sans engagement.* Rosso's choice of title is significant: throughout his life he was sympathetic

Giuseppe Grandi. *Misery.* (date unknown)
Bronze, 12 1/4" high including base
Collection Jack Berizzi, New York

to musicians. As a child he had sung in church choirs.

[15] *Bersagliere con la morosa, Bacio sotto il lampione, Bersagliere con la morosa sotto il lampione.*

[16] *Bersagliere, Tirailleur italien en vedette,* and probably *In esplorazione.*

[17] *Caramel* (*op. cit.,* p. 271) associates this head with a project (now lost) that Rosso entered in a competition launched by the city of Pavia for a monument to Garibaldi. The maquettes were on view October 5–10, 1882. Rosso did not win.

[18] *Il birichino, Dopo una scappata, Il monello, Le gamin, Le gamin parisien.*

[19] See below, pp. 17–18, and note 24.

[20] *Ultimo bacio, Il bacio sulla tomba.*

[21] I first heard of this painting from Professor Giuseppe Prezzolini (see note 58) who gave me the address of its present owner, Mrs. Agnes Surdi, Baldassare Surdi's daughter-in-law. She remembers hearing that it was executed all in one sitting. To her kindness I owe not only the photograph reproduced here, but also Rosso's letter to Surdi (see below, pp. 16–17), the photograph of the *Last Kiss* (p. 16), and the photograph of Rosso's studio (p. 18).

[22] Reprinted in Borghi, *op. cit.,* p. 22.

[23] See note 184.

[24] Although the photograph is inscribed it is, unfortunately, not dated; however, it is safe to say that it must be later than April 27, 1883, but well before Rosso's trip to Paris in 1884.

[25] *Madre e bambino che dormono, Madre e bambino addormentato, Mère et enfant endormis.*

[26] See Luciano Caramel, "I 'ritorni' di Medardo Rosso e due bronzi giovanili," *Commentari,* July–December 1962, pp. 247-53. The only extant version is the bronze in the collection of Cesare Fasola (see note 2). Rosso did not exhibit it in Venice in 1887, but he did show this or another version at the Bodinière, Paris, in 1893.

[27] *La mezzana, La ruffiana, Una megera,* probably *Vieille femme campée au soleil,* and in the Venice National Exhibition of 1887, *Fine.* This, or the *Concierge,* is the *Baucis* in the Paris Salon of 1885.

[28] Rosso was very conscious of the cycles of life, and he used to end his notes to friends with greetings to them and to their "consequence," meaning their children.

[29] *El scior Faust;* in the Paris Salon of 1885 shown under the name *Philémon* (Borghi, *op. cit.,* p. 24).

[30] Certain photographs of Rosso's studio show the shells of negative molds stored on shelves. Some of his sculptures are rare because he neglected to keep either a *modello* or a negative mold of them. For instance, there are only two versions of the *Yvette Guilbert,* one in the Galleria d'Arte Moderna, Rome, and one in the Galleria d'Arte Moderna, Venice.

There is one single wax of *Madame X,* in Venice, and only one bronze of the *Mother and Child Sleeping* (Collection Cesare Fasola) has as yet been discovered. *Modelli* of many of his works are preserved in the private museum in Barzio and in the collection of Mario Vianello Chiodo (see p. 64), Lido, Venice.

[31] The poet Giuseppe Ungaretti vividly remembers Rosso repeating this remark in his Milanese dialect.

[32] *Lo scaccino, Il sacrestano, El grapatt, Se la fuss grappa.* This is a portrait of the old beadle of the church of San Marco in Milan, who was an alcoholic. He looks down at the holy water font, which appears in certain casts, and mumbles to himself: "If only it were grappa!" (the inexpensive Italian *aquavit*).

[33] *Carne altrui, Chair à plaisir, Chair à autrui.*

[34] Borghi, *op. cit.,* fig. 10.

[35] In the twenties, Rosso inscribed a photograph of the *Flesh of Others* to Mario Vianello Chiodo with the remark that it was the first sculpture he had made "around which one could not walk." This could also be said of the earlier *Mother and Child Sleeping* and the *Sacristan.*

[36] *La portinaia, La sciora Orsola,* and in the religious exhibition in Venice in 1921, *Sant'Orsola.* The circumstances of its creation are delightfully told in Rosso's own words: "I couldn't do a thing. The doorkeeper used to scold me; she was a good woman, like a mother. Finally one day I thought, 'Could it be that blasted old creature who keeps me from getting anything done?' Angrily I go down to her room with my clay. I start working fast. I had in mind the effect that she had always made upon me as I went by and looked at her in passing. I managed to snatch that moment from life. It was getting late. I cover the work. I was tired of having my eyes in the clay and of having the old woman's eyes inside me. The next day I lift the wet rags and look. 'This is it! I was satisfied! I had recovered. I had given birth to the *Concierge.*'" Luigi Ambrosini, *Teocrito, Ariosto, minori e minimi,* Milan, Corbaccio, 1926, pp. 365–66.

[37] According to a photograph dated in his hand; cf. Borghi, *op. cit.,* fig. 16.

[38] *Impressione d'Omnibus.*

[39] Dr. Caramel points out that Daumier lithographs were known in Milan; but the one closest to *Impression in an Omnibus* is the lithograph *Train de plaisir de Paris à St.-Germain, wagon de deuxième classe,* 1852, perhaps too much of a caricature to appeal to Rosso, whose subject seems closer to Daumier's paintings or wash drawings of passengers on train benches than to any of his lithographs. Vittore Grubicy, whose collection of photographs after Jean François Millet is still remembered in Milan, would obviously have admired Daumier whether or not in 1878 he happened to see the exhibition of Daumier's paint-

Honoré Daumier. *The First-Class Carriage.* Watercolor. The Walters Art Gallery, Baltimore

ings in Paris. Grubicy traveled constantly and by 1883 he had resided abroad for long periods; his artistic education was cosmopolitan. He may also have owned some small Daumier sculptures or at least had photographs of them, for the latter, more than anything produced in Italy, are close to the style that Rosso was evolving. They were, however, caricatures.

[40] Borghi, *op. cit.*, p. 27. Ardengo Soffici (*Medardo Rosso*, Florence, Vallecchi, 1929, p. 22) speaks of impressions (plural) in an omnibus: *basta guardare una delle sue impressioni d'omnibus.*

[41] Or that he had some subsidy from Count Vittorio Turati, one of his earliest patrons.

[42] Borghi, *op. cit.*, p. 22.

[43] Georges Thomas, or *père* Thomas, was a courageous dealer who, with small capital, backed the artists he believed in, and often accepted the advice of Toulouse-Lautrec.

[44] It was at this gallery that the yearly Exposition Internationale was held, which had been founded by Georges Petit and Giuseppe de Nittis. A great friend of Degas, de Nittis, who had the Paris world at his fingertips and might have been helpful to Rosso, died in 1884.

[45] See below, pp. 53–54.

[46] There is no record of the length of his stay in Paris, nor even of the dates of his arrival and departure. Dr. Giovanni Carandente suggests that he went to Paris *after* the death of his mother (see his entry on Rosso in *Dictionary of Modern Sculpture*, ed. Robert Maillard, New York, Tudor, 1961).

[47] His black moods lasted over long periods and recurred with increasing frequency as he grew older.

[48] This drawing, more refined in its modulation of light and shadow than the portrait of Baldassare Surdi, is now in the private Rosso museum at Barzio.

For years it hung over the bed of Etha Fles, Rosso's patroness. For a detailed account of her role in Rosso's life, see Margaret Scolari Barr, "Medardo Rosso and His Dutch Patroness Etha Fles," *Nederlands Kunsthistorisch Jaarboek*, XIII, 1962, pp. 217–51.

[49] Borghi, *op. cit.*, p. 15.

[50] It is not excluded that he sent sculptures to Paris from Milan, but it is far more likely that he had left works with Gastone Pesce, his old army friend. The catalogue of the Salon of May 1, 1885, lists his entry *Tirailleur italien en vedette* (the *Garibaldino*) under: "Rosso, Melardo [*sic*], chez M. Pesce, Rue Tronchet 23," and in the Salon of 1886, under the same address, he showed his *Gavroche* and *Une mère et son enfant endormis.* After the artist's death in 1928, Gastone Pesce wrote to the Rosso family explaining that even though Rosso was a naturalized French citizen, he had remained, throughout, most loyal to the country of his birth. It is not unreasonable to suspect that it was he who placed Rosso's works in many exhibitions in Paris during the latter's absence from the city from 1884 to 1889.

Funerary Monument to Brusco Onnis. (1888). Bronze, 17 1/2" high. Cimitero Monumentale, Milan

Funerary Monument to Elisa Rognoni
Faini. (1888). Bronze, 19 3/4" high
Cimitero Monumentale, Milan

[51] Nicknamed *El Gessat;* see Borghi, *op. cit.,* fig. 8 right (not "left," as labeled). There is a fine bronze cast in Barzio. In the Cimitero Monumentale in Milan it is unregistered and unfindable.

[52] *Aetas aurea, Età d'oro, Mère et enfant, Mother and Child.* The poetic title calls to mind Rodin's *Age d'airain* of 1876–77.

[53] A photograph of the plaster (Borghi, *op. cit.,* fig. 14 bottom) is inscribed in Rosso's firm hand and small writing of this time: "*Mère et enfant, impression. 1886. Musée du Petit Palais, Paris.*"

[54] See p. 20.

[55] The Trebini head is reproduced in Borghi (*op. cit.,* pl. 6, upper right). The monument to Elisa Rognoni Faini is published in Caramel, "I 'ritorni'. . . ."

[56] Dated 1889 in Borghi (*op. cit.,* pl. 6, upper left). In the Cimitero Monumentale, Milan, *muro di cinta di ponente, no. 4.*

[57] Borghi, *op. cit.,* pl. 8, left. In the Cimitero Monumentale, Milan, *circondante di levante, no. 325.*

[58] An undated Rosso letter among the papers of Professor Giuseppe Prezzolini prescribes that the photograph of the Filippo Filippi monument, three times enlarged, should include the base. It was probably intended for the Impressionist exhibition in the Florence Lyceum in 1910, which Professor Prezzolini helped to organize. Prezzolini was the editor of *La Voce,* which was founded in 1908 (see below, p. 59). Later he became Professor of Italian Literature at Columbia University. His papers regarding Rosso, as well as the complete file of *La Voce* and *Lacerba,* are

in the Casa Italiana of this University. For his brilliant characterization of Rosso, see Barr, *op. cit.,* p. 220, note 4.

[59] Borghi, *op. cit.,* p. 28.

[60] As in 1885, when he had gone briefly to Vienna, where one of his works was acquired by the Hungarian painter Munkácsy.

[61] While transacting the sale of the *Roman Senator* to the Eissler brothers in 1903, Rosso remarked that he had been casting it in Paris while his monument to Filippi was being inaugurated in Milan (see Hans Ankwicz von Kleehoven, "Medardo Rosso a Vienna," *La Biennale di Venezia,* no. 23, January 1955, pp. 23-25). The monument to Filippo Filippi was inaugurated on June 26, 1889 (Borghi, *op. cit.,* p. 75).

[62] Number 305 in the official catalogue of the Exposition Universelle laconically lists "cinq bronzes," with no titles, under "Rosso, Medardo, à Milan."

[63] Borghi, *op. cit.,* p. 75.

[64] *Maternità, Bimbo che poppa.*

[65] Considering how much he treasured his works, it is perhaps significant that he did not save the mother's head to recast it separately. Although Borghi states (*op. cit.,* p. 65) that this *Child at the Breast* was executed in Paris, it might still be an impression of his wife and infant son, begun 1885–86 and cast later in Paris. The course of his life makes it obvious that he was not attached to his wife, who complained a great deal and was never sympathetic to his art. Furthermore, the many warmhearted images of chil-

dren he made during his second Paris period might be accounted for as a parallel or overlapping yearning for his little son and for his own childhood.

[66] *Malato all'ospedale, Dopo la visita, Malade à l'hôpital.*

[67] Edmond Claris, *De l'impressionisme en sculpture*, Paris, Ed. La Nouvelle Revue, 1902, p. 21.

[68] For Italians to go to a public hospital in those days was a traumatic experience. When Rosso was taken to the Sophienspital in Vienna in 1903 he wrote to Wilhelm Bernatzik, "Je suis habitué," alluding, of course, with resignation and self-pity to this first Paris confinement.

[69] These recollections from the records of Mme Ernest Rouart were kindly obtained for me by Mr. and Mrs. John Rewald.

[70] This seems inexact. Rosso's wife was the daughter of a widow. Nino Barbantini (*Medardo Rosso*, Venice, Neri-Pozza, 1950, p. 22) gives a graphic description of the abject poverty of Rosso's brief marital life.

[71] There is no evidence that Rosso saw his wife again after his departure in 1889; according to Mrs. Carlo Carrà, she died in 1933 or 1934.

[72] There is no evidence that Francesco Rosso built a house for his father who, in the 1920's lived in a single room in the Grand Hôtel in Milan.

[73] Posthumously, at the Salon d'Automne, 1929.

[74] Had Rosso been decorated, either in France or Italy, he would have mentioned it, and his son would have documented it.

[75] Could this be the huge plaster *Impression on the Boulevard at Night*, 1895, in reduced form? See below, pp. 46, 48.

[76] Sadi Carnot, President of the Republic, was murdered by an Italian anarchist in Lyons on June 24, 1894.

[77] Toward the end of his life Rosso asked his Venetian friend, Mario Vianello Chiodo, to mail some clippings to a list of friends abroad. The name of Louis Rouart is among them (6, Place St.-Sulpice, Paris), indicating that his friendship extended to other members of the family.

[78] He had become a naturalized French citizen in the illusion that this would make him more acceptable and would bring him commissions.

[79] The talented translator of Hans Christian Andersen as well as Kierkegaard; in a conversation with the author in Rome, 1962.

[80] See Barr, *op. cit.*, p. 238. Professor Verlow remembers that during the first World War, Rosso insistently invited him to witness one of his castings at the dead of night. Verlow refused and Rosso was both astonished and disappointed; he really did need an audience. After the war, every now and then he

cast in bronze in Milan, and Giorgio Nicodemi, sometime Professor of Art History at the University of Milan and editor of *L'Arte*, remembers that Rosso used to remove a gold ring from his finger and throw it in the molten metal because he thought some gold gave the finished bronze finer highlights.

[81] Borghi (*op. cit.*, p. 28) lists some of the amateurs who acquired Rosso's works: Count Armand Doria; the baritone Jean-Baptiste Faure and his relative Mme Noblet; the painters Munkácsy and Roybet are among the recognizable names. Others are Montaignac (employed at the Galeries Georges Petit), Hazard, Grouet, Cahen, Moeller, Albric, Darrier, Babinski, Charles Tillot.

[82] On October 26, 1914, Etha Fles was to write to Nino Barbantini, Director of the Galleria d'Arte Moderna in Venice, "I do realize that they refuse to buy any of the works you like best, but there are others, that everyone can understand" (Archives of the Galleria d'Arte Moderna, Cà Pesaro, Venice).

[83] *Bimba che ride, Bimba ridente.*

[84] *Small Head of Woman Laughing*, also called *Rieuse, Donna ridente*. I retain the French title so as to differentiate it from the *Grande rieuse* of 1891.

[85] Her name seems to have been Bianca Garavaglia, though, if she were truly Spanish, her name would have been spelled otherwise, and could only have sounded this way to Italian ears.

[86] *Donna ridente, Fantesca che ride, Servante rieuse, Large Head of Woman Laughing.*

[87] *Bimbo al sole, Enfant au soleil, Boy in the Sun.*

[88] *Bimbo ebreo, Enfant Juif*, and in the exhibition of religious art in Venice in 1920, *Enfant de Nazareth* and/or *S. Luigi* (Gonzaga).

[89] Borghi, *op. cit.*, p. 27. Correspondence with Baron Philippe de Rothschild and other members of the family in France and England has resulted in consistently negative answers. The portrait is unknown in the family. According to the genealogy given by Frederic Morton in *The Rothschilds* (New York, Atheneum Publishers, 1962) only one Rothschild, Oscar Ruben, born in 1888, would have been of the right age in 1892.

[90] A. Soffici, *Trenta artisti moderni italiani e stranieri*, Florence, Vallecchi, 1950, reproduced on p. 115 with the title *Busto di donna*. This work has not yet come to light and is not listed in the Borghi monograph.

[91] *Medardo Rosso, Impressions* (album published on the occasion of the exhibition at the Eugene Cremetti Gallery, London, 1906), p. 5; see also p. 58.

[92] In conversation with the author, July 1960.

[93] *Fanciullo alle cucine popolari, Bambino alle cucine economiche, Enfant à la bouchée de pain*. A *cucina economica* is a soup kitchen where the poor can

obtain cooked food.

94 *Bimbo malato, Bimbo morente, Enfant malade.*

95 According to Jacques Lipchitz, when Constantin Brancusi first came to Paris he was much interested in Rosso's work. See, for example, the two versions of the *Sleeping Muse* (1906; 1909–10) now in the Musée d'Art Moderne, Paris, or the little marble head of a boy, *Portrait of George* (1911?), in the Guggenheim Museum, New York, and for the inclined neck and domical head, the *Mlle Pogany* (1919–20) in the Arensberg Collection at the Philadelphia Museum of Art.

96 *Conversazione in giardino, L'artista e due signore, Conversation en plein air.*

97 There is no question that the male protagonist represents Rosso himself. The sculpture was executed in Paris (Borghi, *op. cit.*, p. 67) or London (the label in the Galleria d'Arte Moderna, Rome, says London 1893). In a conversation with the author at Barzio Signora Tilde Rosso, the sculptor's daughter-in-law, said that Rosso's meeting with the two ladies took place in London. "There he stood," she remarked, "with his *brioche* [his bulging stomach] before the two ladies. One interested him, the other didn't." However, there is no written evidence of Rosso's having gone to London before 1896.

98 It should be remembered that the taste for *bozzetti* (first sketches in sculpture) developed only in the twentieth century. However, a decade before, Félix Fénéon, in writing of Impressionist painting, had remarked: "The bounding line expresses what is permanent in the object, color what is momentary; the line, a practically abstract boundary, characterizes the object, the unit of color establishes the atmosphere and records the sensation. . . . The new painter of our times [Fénéon was born in Turin in 1844] is willing to make more decisive sacrifices than any of his predecessors. He dares insist on what interests him and he avoids accessory frills.

"If people say of a modern painting, 'It is unfinished,' we reply: 'At what precise moment is a painting "finished"'? The question cannot be answered.

"However, the poor beholder should be left something to do: let us reserve for the painter the severe and controllable task of beginning his paintings and let us reserve for the beholder the advantageous, comfortable, and delightfully comic role of finishing them by his meditations or his dreams." (Félix Fénéon, *Oeuvres*, Paris, Gallimard, 1948, p. 56.)

99 *Dama* (or *Signora*) *dalla veletta, Dame à la voilette, Impression de boulevard.* Two works by Rosso, of which no trace remains, went by the titles *Sortant de l'église* and *Dame au parapluie*; until further evidence, I believe that these were variant titles for this same sculpture. The *Lady with a Veil* and the *Ecce*

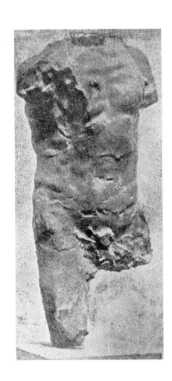

Auguste Rodin. Bronze Torso. (1877)
ABOVE: Petit Palais, Paris
BELOW: Whereabouts unknown

puer were acquired for the Luxembourg in 1907 upon the recommendation of Clemenceau. See below, note 163.

¹⁰⁰ The dates of the successive showings are uncertain, but the second closed on December 19, 1893.

¹⁰¹ It was officially called Théâtre d'Application Bodinier.

¹⁰² The torso that Rodin gave Rosso (page 91, below) was a cast of his study for the *Homme qui marche* (1877); a bronze cast of this study, or of a close variant, is preserved in the Petit Palais, Paris (page 91, above).

In 1910 or shortly afterward, Rosso gave the torso to Gustavo Sforni, one of the most important backers of the First Impressionist Exhibition at the Florence Lyceum in 1910. It remained in Sforni's hands until the second World War, when it was confiscated by the Germans because Sforni was Jewish. It has since disappeared. The *Petite rieuse* is now in the office of Mme Cécile Goldscheider, Director of the Musée Rodin, Paris.

¹⁰³ "Mon cher Rosso, vous m'avez fait un immense plaisir; en arrivant à l'atelier, j'étais frappé d'une folle admiration pour vous. Je ne vous ai pas écrit parceque je ne savais plus votre addresse. Je suis heureux et si samedi vous voulez déjeuner avec moi je serais content. A bientôt, votre ami, Rodin." Address: Monsieur Rosso, statuaire, 15 ou 28 rue Cauchois, Montmartre, Paris (posted in Belleville, Seine-et-Oise). Reproduced in Giovanni Papini, *Medardo Rosso* (Arte moderna italiana), Milan, Hoepli, 1945, p. 11.

¹⁰⁴ At a time when Rodin was inventing and discarding sketch upon sketch for his Balzac monument, the contemplation of Rosso's spontaneous works and his conversation must have been refreshing. Rodin had read all Balzac's works in order to prepare himself for the portrait. The following passage from the *Chef-d'oeuvre inconnu* is singularly harmonious with Rosso's abolition of sharp contours and his interest in atmospheric effects:

"The human body is not defined by lines. From this point of view sculptors can approach the truth better than we painters [it is the old painter Frenhofer who is speaking]: nature contains a succession of rotundities that are enveloped one into the other. There are no lines in nature where everything is full; it is in modeling that one draws, thereby detaching things from the environment in which they are; only the distribution of light brings out the appearance of the body. I have spread over the contours a cloud of blond and warm half-tones so that one cannot put one's finger precisely on the place where the contours meet the background. Seen close, the work seems cottony and lacking in exactness, but seen at

Rodin. *Monument to Balzac*

a distance of two steps, everything becomes firm, stands still, and detaches itself; the body turns, the air circulates all around it. Perhaps one should not draw a single line but attack the figure from the center, concentrating first on the more lighted protuberances and later passing on to the darker portions. Doesn't the sun proceed in this way?"

¹⁰⁵ Rodin's diaries are not open to scholars. Louis Vauxcelles implies that they saw each other often (see note 129). The Rosso papers in Barzio are in the private possession of the sculptor's heirs and could not be examined by the author.

¹⁰⁶ *L'uomo alle corse, The Sportsman.*

¹⁰⁷ See the reminiscences of Louis Rouart, above, p. 30.

¹⁰⁸ *Uomo che legge il giornale, Homme qui lit, Reading,* and in the Venice exhibition of 1914, *Monsieur X.* The fact that the *Monsieur X* in the catalogue of the 1914 Biennale is the *Man Reading* is established by a letter of November 3, 1914, from Etha Fles to Nino Barbantini, preserved in the files of the Galleria d'Arte Moderna, Venice.

¹⁰⁹ Yvette Guilbert, *The Song of My Life*, London, George Harrap, 1929, pp. 102ff. Many portraits of the great singer are reproduced in this book, but Rosso's head does not appear. Since it was not a commissioned portrait, Yvette Guilbert may never have seen it; or, if she did, she may not have thought it sufficiently flattering. Perhaps Rosso should have offered her a cast, for she does complain that Toulouse-Lautrec never gave her a single drawing or sketch of the many he made of her.

¹¹⁰ This interpretation probably derives from Ar-

FROM LEFT TO RIGHT: Detail of *Conversation in the Garden, Bookmaker, Man Reading*

dengo Soffici's comments on the head (*Trenta artisti ...*, p. 103). It should be borne in mind that Rosso loved music and was always attracted to musicians. He had executed the bust to the music critic Filippo Filippi out of sheer friendship, with no remuneration (see above, p. 28). In the 1920's, Umberto Giordano, the composer of *Andrea Chénier*, was one of his closest friends. Rosso compared his *Ecce puer* to Bach's eighth prelude. He used to sing to Etha Fles, who especially remembered a Jewish song that he had somehow mastered.

[111] The motif of the blurred or extinguished right eye recurs in Picasso's bronzes, *Head of Alice Derain* (1905) and *Head of Fernande* (1905), both of which are meant to be seen with the subject's left eye closer to the beholder so that the right side of the face slips away in a fugitive perspective. Violent facial asymmetries occur as early as 1899 in Bourdelle's *Head of Beethoven* and later in Matisse's sculptures. This is not to suggest a direct influence of Rosso (although Mr. John Richardson informs me that Picasso remembers Rosso's work admiringly) because neither in 1900 (Exposition Universelle) nor in 1904 (Salon d'Automne) did he exhibit his *Yvette Guilbert, Madame Noblet,* or *Madame X*; it is rather to imply that these inventions of his, formulated in the nineteenth century, became part of the artistic vocabulary of the twentieth.

[112] *Parigi di notte, Coppie danzanti, Impression de boulevard la nuit, Impression Place de Clichy.*

[113] In his reminiscences, Louis Rouart alludes to an ivory "Place de Clichy in the snow at one o'clock in the morning" (see above, p. 30). The subject might be the same, but it is hard to believe that Rosso ever *carved,* even on a small scale. Perhaps Louis Rouart knew the work only through photographs. None of Rosso's works are listed in the Rouart sales catalogue.

[114] Letters to the Mayor of Jessains inquiring about the Noblet family and about the plaster cast have not been answered.

[115] There is no knowing whether Rosso was actually inspired by a woman called Dolores, or whether he and Etha Fles had fallen into the habit of calling the head this way. As for the title *Madame X*, Rosso was affected by the late-nineteenth-century fashion for anonymity and mysteriousness; there are portraits by Degas, Sargent, Rodin, and many others which go by this title.

[116] Borghi, *op. cit.*, p. 69.

[117] The publication of the Biennale catalogues follows a system in which a first edition is issued in time for the opening, then errors are rectified in subsequent printings during the course of the summer. The date 1896 for *La signora X* remains constant in all the editions of the 1914 Biennale catalogue.

[118] See below, pp. 58–59.

[119] See Barr, *op. cit.*, p. 240.

[120] In a conversation with the author in the summer of 1960. Zervos remembers Rosso well.

[121] He did not exhibit it in the Florence Lyceum show in 1910, when he had full freedom to enter whatever he wished.

[122] Knud Verlow in reminiscing about Paris in the first World War said that Rosso saw a great deal of Modigliani; unfortunately he remembered no details that would make this friendship, heretofore unmen-

tioned, more vivid for us. Through Modigliani Rosso might well have met Brancusi.

[123] The fact that the Venice wax is unique, that Rosso never recast it, and that no *modello* of it exists proves beyond much doubt that he coated the *modello* itself with wax.

[124] Francesco Rosso must have been conscious of the fact that everyone knew that his father's inventive vein had come to an end. As Professor Prezzolini remarked in reminiscing about the Florence Lyceum show, "By 1910 he had done nothing new for years." See below, note 146.

[125] The Noblets, who were related to the baritone Jean-Baptiste Faure, an avid collector, owned the *Concierge, Golden Age, Lady with a Veil,* and perhaps the large *Impression on the Boulevard at Night.*

[126] A drawing of himself in shirt sleeves at a desk, in which he is noticeably portly, bears the date 1896 and the letterhead of a hotel in Piccadilly Circus (p. 82).

[127] I am informed by Dr. Albert Elsen that the *Balzac* was cast in bronze only after Rodin's death.

[128] Mme Goldscheider suggests that the idea of the figure wrapped in a monkish robe came to Rodin from a Japanese figurine; see Cécile Goldscheider, "La genèse d'une oeuvre: Le Balzac de Rodin," *Revue des Arts,* II, 1, March 1952, p. 44.

In her recent book, *Rodin, sa vie, son oeuvre, son héritage* (Paris, Les productions de Paris, 1962–63), she reproduces a small preparatory study in clay for the *Balzac* which in corpulence, in stance, in cohesion to the ground seems close to the male figure in the *Conversation.* See also Albert Elsen, *Rodin,* New York, The Museum of Modern Art, 1963, pp. 89ff.

[129] Whether the artists were already cordial friends before Rodin's note of January 1894 and whether they frequented one another afterward cannot be verified in contemporary writings, but the critic Louis Vauxcelles had no doubts on the matter. In his preface to Rosso's posthumous retrospective at the Salon d'Automne of 1929, he rose—not for the first time to Rosso's defense:

"I knew him. He was a red-haired giant—a Dionysus or rather a Hephaistus. Formidable in appearance, he was as strong as a Turk, as good as bread, and candid as a child.

"This extraordinary personage, the most important Italian sculptor since Gemito, was a precursor who subverted the sacred principles of traditional statuary, a revolutionary who opened out a path heretofore unexplored. He, with Carrière, influenced Rodin most fruitfully. Without Medardo Rosso (and we feel justified in stating this), Rodin would never have executed his *Balzac* as he [ultimately] conceived

it. And Rodin was fully aware of this, because twenty thousand times he watched his colleague at work in his studio and listened to him and exchanged his *Torso* in return for the *Rieuse* and coldly utilized his discoveries. The great—in the wake of Shakespeare and Molière—take what they want wherever they find it."

[130] Of particular interest regarding the Rodin-Rosso controversy are the remarks of Aurel, *Rodin devant la femme,* Paris, Maison du Livre, 1919. Aurel is the nom de plume of Mme Aurélie Mortier de Faucamberge, b. 1882. She was a friend and admirer of Rodin's, although she managed at the same time to be on such good terms with Rosso that he gave her a *Concierge* (this information through the kindness of Mr. and Mrs. Harry L. Winston). A few months before Rodin's death, Mme Aurel asked him about Rosso; he answered, "Too late." He was already weakened by illness. In the same year, she questioned Rosso about Rodin. He answered: "I have nothing to say. When I want an object I go to the factory. An artist has no branch shops [*succursales*]. One must be on the right path. Rodin is still on the path of a trade. He makes statues. There are no statues. Nothing is a statue." Rosso told her that he and Rodin had planned their exchange of works in London in 1896. In Mme Aurel's book, the chapter that concerns Rosso is entitled "L'Initiateur."

Professor Nicodemi remembers that when he and the critic Ugo Ojetti called on Rodin in 1912 they dropped a studied, casual question about Rosso. The great man replied that he had never heard of him.

[131] The distinguished actress, then Mrs. Brünhof.

Vincent van Gogh. *Diligence de Tarascon.* (1889) Collection Henry Pearlman, New York

[132] Rosso did a drawing that he or his son titled *Impressione Caffè la Roche a Parigi* (p. 82). This might be Rosso's abbreviation for the Café La Rochefoucauld frequented by Degas.

[133] Both Degas and Lautrec were well-known figures in Montmartre, Rosso's own *quartier*.

[134] During *père* Tanguy's lifetime Rosso acquired from him van Gogh's *Diligence de Tarascon*, for this picture is not listed in the catalogue of the Tanguy sale of June 2, 1894 (I owe this information to Mr. John Rewald). In 1895 Rosso gave it to his disciple Milo Beretta who took it back with him to Montevideo. From London, on July 13, 1906 (just nine days after he had met Maurice Denis), Rosso wrote Beretta the following letter in French:
"My friend,

I wrote you a short while ago (as always) and without answer—Anyway I've allowed myself to be ——again [the dash is Rosso's] You write me about your situation and I answer you immediately—But I write you to get news of you and you tell me nothing—

Today I also write to tell you that of the works you have—only one which I gave you—

Knowing well its great merit—but to give you pleasure I did not fail—[scribbles] the carriage of Tarascon [illegible]

This work only today costs some twenty thousand fr.

Of this I warn you so that you may make your parents understand that you haven't had bad friends —

Who can inform you of this value and know that you were right to make them spend a little for Paris for you have made yourself a certain intelligence which in the end everyone pays for

I

Am here for my affairs [illegible] this last stage will come to an end this year

Yours, all yours, always yours

your

ROSSO"

Louis Piérard, who in 1909 had written a short monograph on Rosso, saw the painting in an exhibition in Buenos Aires. He wrote about it to J. B. de la Faille. It is now in the collection of Mr. Henry Pearlman, New York, to whose courtesy I owe a photocopy of the letter as well as other documentation.

[135] [Unsigned], "Editorial: Medardo Rosso 1858–1928," *Burlington Magazine*, October 1950, pp. 277–78.

[136] If the heirs of Mrs. Tilde Rosso open the Barzio archives to scholars, some further information on Rosso's Paris contacts may come to light.

[137] In later years when a friend asked him why he did not do something new, he broke forth, "If you love me, don't wish that on me. I suffer so much physically when I create, that in those hours it is as if my flesh were being torn from my bones" (Fles, *Mensch und Künstler*, p. 35).

[138] Vittore Grubicy was by then very deaf and his brother Alberto acted to an extent as his lieutenant, and must have been in Paris as Segantini's dealer.

[139] Discounting the destroyed *Last Kiss* of 1882–83, the *Impression on the Boulevard at Night* was Rosso's first attempt to render human figures life-size from head to foot. His *Madame X* and *Madame Noblet*, as well as his later *Ecce puer* (1906–7), all over life-size, are proof of his interest in a large scale. However, it is possible that the dimensions of Rosso's portrait of Dr. Fles were established by Miss Fles who may have intended to place it as a memorial to her father in a hospital or as a monument in a square of Utrecht.

[140] Curt Seidel, "L'arte di Medardo Rosso," *L'Artista moderno*, x, March 10, 1911, p. 86.

[141] Veth's etching is reproduced in Barr, *op. cit.*, p. 224, fig. 7.

[142] Miss Agatha Verkroost, Etha Fles's adopted daughter, remarked (in a letter to the author) that the family did not like it, and that it was allowed to disintegrate.

[143] Dr. Georg Treu, Director of the Albertinum in Dresden and a classical scholar interested in modern art, had casts of some of the heads from the Pergamon Altar in his house (this information through the kindness of Mrs. Sibyl Moholy-Nagy). He bought a wax of the *Sick Boy* (dated 1901 by the Museum) and a head of Vitellius (acquired by the Museum in 1903), both now in the Staatliche Kunstsammlungen, Dresden, and wrote that Rosso more than Rodin was a painter in sculpture (quoted in the Cremetti album). This *Vitellius* (p. 76) is the only important bronze copy after the antique by Rosso that has as yet been identified.

[144] Used by Miss Fles in her history of art, and for the catalogues of the Artaria show in Vienna and the Eugene Cremetti show in London.

[145] For this incident and for Rosso's two stays in Vienna, in 1903 and 1905, see von Kleehoven, *op. cit.*

[146] As already mentioned, Rosso had slowed down long before; but the seizure of 1903 may be the first recorded symptom of some illness that had gradually set in. Etha Fles in her many effusive writings about Rosso never alludes to his health (cf. Barr, *op. cit.*, p. 243, note 55). Professor Nicodemi, who knew Rosso and remembers a great deal about him, does not believe that he came to a halt though he offers no evidence; he thinks that every now and then Rosso

Head of Vitellius. (Acquired by the Dresden museum 1903). Bronze, 12 1/4" high. Staatliche Skulpturensammlungen, Dresden

undertook a portrait but did not keep a *modello* of it and did not duplicate it. Photographs or documentation of such dispersed works may come to light when the Rosso papers at Barzio are made accessible to scholars.

[147] See above, note 61.

[148] The Salon d'Automne was founded in 1903 under the auspices of Carrière. Rosso, as one of its founders, was commemorated shortly after his death by a one-man show in the Salon d'Automne of 1929.

[149] Unfortunately, his entries are not itemized and are listed in the catalogue merely as "Impressions (bronze et cire)." Reviews mention many works that can be identified, but also a *Pierreuse* (prostitute) which may be either the *Flesh of Others* with a more Parisian title, or a work that has since disappeared. Profesor Nicodemi (in a letter to the author) thinks he remembers that the *Pierreuse* had a kerchief around her neck.

[150] Prince Paul Troubetzkoy, eight years younger than Rosso, had received his artistic education in Milan, and for a while (three years after Rosso had been expelled because he demanded live models) had followed the courses at the Brera Academy. He had worked under the painter Ranzoni and the sculptor Grandi, who were, environmentally, Rosso's ancestors, being anti-academic and "impressionist" in tendency. Appointed to the State Art School in Moscow, he had scrapped the old plaster casts and had insisted on holding life classes. When he exhibited in the

First International Exhibition in Venice in 1895, though six years younger than Rosso, he had already executed important public monuments. In 1900, he had received a Grand Prix in Paris, and the Luxembourg had bought his *Tolstoy on Horseback*. Though Troubetzkoy freely admitted having learned a great deal from Rosso in Milan, by 1904 Rosso resented him. In this same Salon, Troubetzkoy had sixty-five entries.

[151] Rodin had no entries in this exhibition.

[152] Rosso felt that he could best assert himself by compelling the beholder to see his work in relation to that of other artists, present and past. Since among the living, his greatest rival was Rodin, he invited comparison between his *Man in the Hospital* and Rodin's *Balzac*. He also used as "comparison pieces" certain copies of Renaissance or classical works, labeling them "Donatello" or "Michelangelo" with no further elucidation. See also note 156.

[153] Both notices are reprinted, with scanty documentation, in the Cremetti album. On page 22 there is a quote from a *Gil Blas* of 1904 in which Vauxcelles considers Rosso a sculpting painter, compares him to Carrière, and says that Rosso was submerged by Rodin as Verrocchio had been by Michelangelo. On page 27, Stéphane Cloud is quoted, from *L'Europe artiste* of December 1904: "Rosso is the greatest sculptor of modern Italy and one of the greatest in the contemporary world."

[154] It is probably through the Rouarts that Rosso

made the acquaintance of Harald Gutherz whose mother is still remembered in Austria as a lady of great cultivation deeply interested in the arts. As a wedding present Rosso gave Gutherz a bronze cast of his *Gavroche* (see Giorgio Nicodemi, "Le Gamin souriant e cinque lettere di Medardo Rosso," *Emporium,* LXXXIII, 1936, pp. 296–302).

[155] A. F. Seligmann, the more conservative critic of the *Neue Freie Presse* (reprinted in *Kunst und Künstler von Gestern und Heute,* ed. Konegen, Vienna, 1910), makes fun of Rosso's anxieties about correct light, and remarks that the vitrines or "cages" in which Rosso enclosed his works performed the function of frames.

[156] Dr. Caramel visited Barzio in May 1962 and re-examined the comparison pieces. He found plaster casts (not copies by Rosso) of an Etruscan bearded head, a head that he considers a Vitellius, a little Egyptian head, a small female nude somewhat in the manner of Renoir; a small copy in plaster by Rosso of what he believes to be Donatello's marble *David* in the Museo Nazionale, Florence; a copy, perhaps by Rosso, of Michelangelo's *Madonna* in the Medici Chapel; a torso, which Dr. Caramel considers a direct cast from an antique fragment. In my notes, taken in 1960, I associated this with the Rodin torso because of the broken legs of different lengths. A somewhat Etruscan plaster head with beard and curls is preserved in Miss Agatha Verkroost's collection in Bergen (kindly photographed by Mr. and Mrs. Harry Winston). A copy of the head of Donatello's *St. Francis* in Sant'Antonio, Padua, appears in photographs of Rosso's studio (identified by Dr. Leo Steinberg); see p. 36, second from right. Many fragments found by Francesco Rosso when he closed his father's studio in 1928 are set in the surround of the door of the private museum in Barzio. Other objects collected by the sculptor may be preserved by the Rosso family, for instance, a set of Chinese figurines mentioned to me by Giuseppe Ungaretti which appear on the little table in the photograph of Etha Fles in her studio, Rome, 1908 (p. 78).

[157] All efforts to ascertain which member of the Lanckoroński family this may have been have proved fruitless.

[158] See Barr, *op. cit.,* pp. 233–34.

[159] I am indebted to Mrs. May Cippico for the correct identification of this portrait. I quote the pertinent passages of her letter dated September 13, 1961: "I recognized the photograph at once as being the portrait of my brother Alfred William Mond as a very young boy, about five or six years of age, I think circa 1906 or 1907. . . . The wax model [*sic*] was in our home in Hyde Park Square certainly until after 1918. The bust was certainly not in the house at the time of my mother's death (1941) and I have no idea of what became of it."

[160] In this connection it is worth noting the remarks of Edmond Claris (*op. cit.,* p. 26): "The first time I saw him [about 1901, after the portrait of Dr. Fles, which he calls "merveilleux et grassement coloré"], he placed himself in the exact spot where he had posed a woman whose portrait he was doing. Then, removing the wet cloth that covered the clay, which was still damp, he asked me to tell him frankly how this woman struck me. I shall always remember his joy when, after having described to him the character that emanated from the face I had under my eyes and the feelings that seemed to animate it, I declared to him that this simply modeled clay gave me the impression of a blonde, with golden hair and a white, milky complexion." This proves that in 1901 Rosso was modeling a new head (he would hardly have been duplicating one of his former sculptures in clay), and the description brings to mind the *Head of a Young Woman* (p. 79), now at the Peridot Gallery, which formerly belonged to Alberto Capozzi, an agent of the Grubicy brothers in Paris.

[161] In conversation with the author at Barzio, August 1960.

[162] Etha Fles and Ardengo Soffici speak of the *Ecce puer* as Rosso's last work. The Borghi monograph, however, suggests that it was followed seven years later by the *Madame X* of 1913 (see above, p. 49).

[163] In 1920, when Rosso wrote the French statesman to protest that these works had not been put back on view since the war, he addressed him as "mon cher et grand ami." However, Clemenceau replied through a secretary that he could not interfere in the arrangements of the Luxembourg. The *Ecce puer* wax was damaged when the collections of the Luxembourg were relocated in other museums. In 1928 when Francesco Rosso came to Paris to close his father's studio, he gave a bronze *Ecce puer* to the Luxembourg, which is now preserved by the Musée National d'Art Moderne (not on view in 1962). The wax of the *Lady with the Veil* is in the Lyons museum as a "dépôt de l'Etat."

[164] Some remarks by Apollinaire under the pseudonym Paracelse on Ardengo Soffici (reprinted for the first time in Guillaume Apollinaire, *Chroniques d'art, 1902–1918,* ed. L.-C. Breunig, Paris, Gallimard, 1960, p. 439) give evidence of the interest he aroused on the international scene in full war time:

". . . *La Ghirba* [the newspaper of the 5th Italian Army at the front] publishes caricatures by lieutenant Ardengo Soffici, powerful caricatures made of cut-out newspaper columns. They are all the more expressive thanks to this simple and unexpected medium.

Etha Fles in Rome, 1908—9
From left to right: *Concierge, Baby Chewing Bread, Ecce puer, Gavroche,*
Grande rieuse, Child in the Sun, Lady with a Veil, Bookmaker, Little Girl Laughing,
Sick Boy, The Golden Age, Jewish Boy, Man in the Hospital

"Ardengo Soffici is not unknown in Paris. Both writer and artist, he was the decorator of the *La Plume* publications. . . . Ardent and restless, he introduced into Italy the most daring and remarkable artists of the past generation; among others, he presented Degas, Cézanne, Henri Rousseau, Matisse, Picasso, Braque. He was also a defender of Rosso. Loyal, independent, and unmercenary, he belongs through bonds of friendship to the small band of poet-critics such as Guillaume Apollinaire, André Salmon, Roger Allard, who succeeded in defending with conviction the painters of the new generations who were forsaken by professional criticism."

[165] See note 102.

[166] I have been unable to locate a catalogue of the exhibition.

[167] Having obtained a pass from a curator, he arrived at the museum early in the morning, put up one of his pieces on a base, and waited for the visitors to be admitted. As they did not reveal surprise at the presence of his sculpture in the same room with Michelangelo, he felt that he had won his point (see Soffici, *Medardo Rosso,* p. 15). According to Barban-

tini (*op. cit.,* p. 11), he placed his *Baby Chewing Bread* close to Michelangelo's *David,* and younger museum visitors preferred the *Baby.*

[168] In conversations with Mario Vianello Chiodo, he harped on the inhumanity of the Futurists.

[169] Quoted in Gino Severini, *Tutta la vita di un pittore,* Cernusco sul Naviglio, Garzanti, 1946, p. 133. For a report of this exhibition, see pp. 128-38. Severini was taken to call on Rosso by Soffici and Boccioni (*ibid.,* p. 142).

[170] He was born in Rome in 1880 and spent his early years there.

[171] Than the work of Meunier, Bourdelle, and Rodin whom Boccioni discussed in the preceding paragraphs.

[172] Umberto Boccioni, *Pittura, scultura futuriste* (*dinamismo plastico*), Milan, Edizioni futuriste di "Poesia," 1914, pp. 397, 399-401.

[173] Roberto Longhi, *Scritti giovanili, 1912—1922,* Florence, Sansoni, 1961, p. 162.

[174] Reproduced in Carola Giedion-Welcker, *Contemporary Sculpture,* New York, Wittenborn, 1961, p. 76.

[175] Apollinaire, *op. cit.*, pp. 437—38 (reprinted from *L'Europe nouvelle*, July 13, 1918).

[176] Since this article is not listed in the Borghi bibliography, it can be inferred that it is not among the Rosso papers in Barzio. It is impossible to ascertain whether in July 1918 Rosso was still in Paris or back in Milan. Etha Fles, who always kept an eye on the press, was in Switzerland.

[177] When his son and daughter-in-law went to Paris to close his studio after his death, they found the mass of clay dried out and empty.

[178] The precise date cannot be ascertained because of contradictory evidence.

[179] Rosso was born on June 21, the name day of this obscure child saint.

[180] The Marinoni family, to which Margherita Sarfatti was related.

[181] It was probably at this exhibition that she introduced Rosso to Mussolini. The Duce examined his works and Rosso laconically remarked, "Voilà." In 1931 Mussolini was to buy the *Ecce puer* and the *Lady with the Veil*, the same pieces that had been selected by Clemenceau in 1907. The sculptor's son Francesco used the money to establish a Medardo Rosso prize at the Brera Academy, from which his father had been expelled. Rosso's feelings about Fascism are not ascertainable; of Mussolini he remarked:

"He laughs well. He allows himself to be photographed a great deal. But he should look at the faces of those who surround him, at his friends, at those who love him too much" (Ambrosini, *op. cit.*, p. 364).

[182] The most important dissenting voice in Rosso's critical revival of the twenties was that of Benedetto Croce. In the Prezzolini archives there is a letter from Rosso to Dolores Prezzolini, postmarked October 25, 1921, that requests the address of the "philosopher-moralist Benedetto Croce who surely keeps regular hours for lunch and dinner." Croce had favorably reviewed the book of a young sculptor and university graduate (Michele Guerrisi, *Dei valori ideali e pratici nella storia dell'arte*, Naples, Errico, 1920), quoting passages from it in which Rosso and Meštrović were accused of turning out works with the intent of attracting notice by arousing astonishment, and of posing as victims of their own artistic ideals; reprinted in Benedetto Croce, *La critica e la storia delle arti figurative*, Bari, Laterza, 1934; 2nd ed., 1946, pp. 194—96.

[183] Carlo Carrà, *La mia vita*, Milan, Rizzoli, 1943, p. 277.

[184] The contrast between the many letters Rosso wrote after 1906 and his note to Mr. Surdi of 1883 cannot be accounted for merely by the gap of twenty-

Head of a Young Woman. (1901?)
Wax over plaster, 15 3/4" high
Peridot Gallery, New York

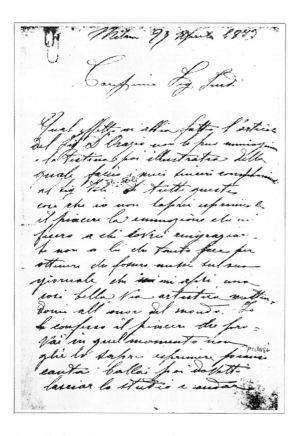

Page of a letter from Rosso to Baldassare Surdi,
April 27, 1883

Page of a letter written by Rosso in the 1920's

three years, even though most handwritings change
with the passage of time. The script of the early letter is small, wiry, and neat, the lines straight and
evenly separated; the writing of the later letters is
larger, wildly irregular, full of scratched-out letters
or words, often illegible. The flow of thought in the
early letter is colloquial but not illogical, the later
letters and published writings are disconnected, repetitious, full of mental short cuts, obscure allusions,
and returns to previous ideas. No letters for the in-
tervening years have come to light, but the change
in handwriting denotes a change in eyesight and in
the response of the hand, while the broken line of
thought suggests some unsteadiness in the mechan-
ics of the mind. Whether these alterations, physical
and psychological, occurred as a result of the accident in 1903 or by degrees between Rosso's twenty-
fifth and forty-eighth years is a mystery that will
probably never be solved.

[185] The Museum of Modern Art's *Concierge* is dedicated to Umberto Giordano.

[186] Rosso is buried in the Cimitero Monumentale
in Milan (*campo 4 acattolici, no. 119*). A bronze cast
of the *Ecce puer* stands as his monument, with the
words *Fine di una vita e principio di un'arte* (end of
a life and beginning of an art).

Appendix: Rosso's Drawings

The bulk of Medardo Rosso's drawings is in the Rosso Museum at Barzio.* By far the most important is the life-size portrait of his mother on her deathbed (November 11—12, 1884; page 21) which, because of the chiaroscuro modeling, may be compared to the portrait of Baldassare Surdi (April 1883, page 17). This is a "finished drawing" intended to be seen as an independent work of art; the same cannot be said of the other, far smaller drawings, most of which are on hotel or café note paper, some in pencil, some in ink or ink and wash, and some in crayon.

In fact, in his drawings, Rosso continued to be a painter as, with quick agility, he set down his impressions of landscapes, beaches, city squares, people walking on the streets, loafing in bars or cafés, or working in the kitchen. Often, in the solitude of hotel rooms, he drew himself—combing his hair, sitting at his desk (page 82), or packing a suitcase.

The drawings present technical differences depending on the texture of the paper and the medium he used. In some, the touch of the pencil is undiscernible; they are as granulated and powdery as Seurat's. Others are nervously hatched in insistent, electric, zigzag strokes. Strong *repoussoirs* and light effects, a sensitive gradation of values as well as calculated steep perspectives make one realize how much mastery of the strictly pictorial language he sacrificed when he dedicated himself exclusively to sculpture. Many of these sketches could have been elaborated into original canvases; one cannot but sense in them Rosso's sporadic temptation to revert to painting.

Only for the rare portrait drawings and perhaps for a reclining nude seen from the back did Rosso use a model; in all other cases the impromptu character of his notations endow them with the freshness of a diary of what caught his eye's fancy. We wander with him from Trafalgar Square (below) to an Alpine landscape, from restaurants (page 82) and billiard rooms (page 83) to the flat Dutch countryside and the seaside near Hendaye.

Perhaps the happiest of his inventions is the drawing of a horse going uphill (page 83). Sitting high beside the cabdriver, Rosso looked down on the rump of the horse, which, with the shafts, fills more than half the sheet; the horse's ears are profiled against the white of the rising road edged by trees. It is a vision of exceptional daring that proves beyond a doubt Rosso's understanding of the most advanced painting of the turn of the century.

* Fifty drawings, all in Barzio, are listed in the Mino Borghi monograph. Some few others are in the collections of Dr. Gianni Mattioli, Milan; Carlo Carrà, Milan; and Ardengo Soffici, Poggio a Caiano (Florence); and two are in the Peridot Gallery, New York.

Trafalgar Square. Peridot Gallery, New York

At the Café La Roche. Rosso Museum, Barzio

The Artist at His Desk. Rosso Museum, Barzio

Carriage Horse Going Uphill. Rosso Museum, Barzio

Billiard Players. Rosso Museum, Barzio

Chronology

1858 Born Turin, June 21; father Domenico, station-master; mother Luigia Bono of better family.

1870 Family moves to Milan.

1879 Enters army; stationed at Pavia, Rome.

1882 Mustered out of army. May 3: enrolls in the Brera Academy.

1883 March 29: expelled from the Brera Academy. April: goes to Rome for Esposizione Belle Arti where he exhibits 4 works. April 27: back in Milan.

1884 To Paris. Assistant to Dalou; meets Rodin. Returns to Milan. November 11: mother dies.

1885 April 16: marries Giuditta Pozzi; November 22: son Francesco born. Short trip to Vienna, sells to the Hungarian painter Munkácsy.

1886– Sculptures shown at the Paris Salon and at the
1889 Indépendants. In Milan does posthumous portraits for funerary monuments.

1887 To Venice; exhibits in Esposizione Internazionale Artistica.

1889 Before June 26: leaves Milan for Paris; shows in Exposition Universelle. Becomes ill, goes to Lariboisière Hospital. A sculpture of his in the window of *père* Thomas attracts attention of Henri Rouart who befriends him.

1893 Death of *père* Tanguy, from whom Rosso had acquired van Gogh's *Diligence de Tarascon*. November–December: exhibits in the foyer of the Bodinière.

1894 January 17: Rodin writes enthusiastic note to Rosso whose studio he had recently visited.

1895 Gives van Gogh's *Diligence de Tarascon* to his disciple Milo Beretta who takes it home with him to Montevideo.

1896 To London for exhibition at Boussod and Valadon with Pre-Raphaelites.

1898 Plaster of Rodin's Balzac shown at Société Nationale des Beaux-Arts; Rosso convinced he has influenced Rodin's conception.

1900 Rejected by Italian Commissioners for Exposition Universelle, manages to exhibit in Segantini's gallery thanks to Alberto Grubicy, Segantini's dealer. Meets Etha Fles who becomes his patroness; goes to Utrecht to execute portrait of her father and for a circulating Impressionist exhibition in which he is featured.

1901 Proceeds to Germany for exhibitions of his work. Returns to Paris. Edmond Claris visits his studio, sees him modeling portrait of a blond woman.

1902 Georg Treu, Director of Albertinum, Dresden, buys *Sick Boy* for the museum.

1903 Before January 17: on way to Vienna Secession is carried unconscious to Sophienspital (Westbahnhof), Vienna; then moves to Hôtel de France, Vienna, where he remains until June 8. July 1: to Leipzig, Berlin, Brussels, where he has relapse. Returns to Paris. Is one of the *fondateurs* of the Salon d'Automne.

1904 One-man show at the Salon d'Automne; seen by the painter and writer Ardengo Soffici who later becomes his propagandist in Italy.

1905 Before February 10: to Vienna for one-man show at Kunsthaus Artaria.

1906 February–March: To London; shows in second section of International Society at New Gallery. December–January: One-man show at Cremetti Gallery, London. Portrait of Alfred William Mond, the *Ecce puer*, executed in this year or early in 1907.

1907 Returns to Paris at uncertain date. Clemenceau arranges to have *Lady with a Veil* and *Ecce puer* bought for the Luxembourg.

1908 December 20: first issue of Soffici's periodical *La Voce* (Florence) contains piece on Rosso. Etha Fles moves from Paris to Rome.

1909 Soffici publishes *Il caso Medardo Rosso*. Plans for Impressionist exhibition in Florence initiated. December 15: Gustavo Sforni, important backer of projected exhibition in Florence, calls on Rosso in Paris.

1910 To Florence for *Prima Mostra dell'Impressionismo*, Florence, which opens April 20.

1911 April 13: opening of Esposizione Internazionale di Belle Arti, Rome, in which Rosso participates. At unascertained date between 1909–11 is reunited with his son Francesco.

1912 February 5–24: exhibition of Futurist painters at Bernheim-Jeune, Paris. After April 11: Boccioni sends his *Technical Manifesto of Futurist Sculpture* to Rosso; produces sculpture inspired by Rosso.

1913 March 29: Etha Fles in Turin with Rosso offers some of his work to the Museo Civico.

1914 April 17: attends his one-man show at Venice Biennale. July 31: Galleria d'Arte Moderna, Rome, buys *Lady with a Veil* and accessions 3 gifts from Etha Fles. August 3: outbreak of World War I. Fall: Galleria d'Arte Moderna, Venice, buys *Ecce puer* and accessions 3 gifts from Etha Fles and 3 from Rosso.

1915 February 21, or shortly after: Rosso room inaugurated in Galleria d'Arte Moderna, Venice. May 24: Italy declares war on Austria. At uncertain date Rosso returns to Paris, frequents Knud Verlow, Modigliani.

1916 August 16: Boccioni dies.

1917 Madame Aurel, Rodin eulogist, calls on Rosso. October: Italians defeated by Austrians at Caporetto; Rosso leaves for Italy at uncertain date. November 17: Rodin dies.

1918 November 4: Armistice with Austria.

1920 September—October: participates in exhibition of religious art, Palazzo Reale, Venice. Writes Clemenceau complaining that his 2 sculptures have not been reinstalled in Luxembourg.

1921 February 24: his letter to Clemenceau published in *Gazzetta di Venezia*. Meets Margherita Sarfatti in Venice.

1922 Mussolini's March on Rome.

1923 March 24—April 8: one-man show at Bottega di Poesia, Milan.

1926 January 12: article "Concepimento—Limite—Infinito" published in *L'Ambrosiano* (Milan). February—March: shows in *Prima Mostra del Novecento*, Milan. Margherita Sarfatti introduces him to Mussolini. Is represented in exhibition of modern Italian painting, Grand Central Art Galleries, New York.

1928 March 31: dies in Milan at the age of 69.

1929 November: retrospective exhibition at the Salon d'Automne, Paris.

1930 Included in Royal Academy exhibition of Italian art, Burlington House, London.

1931 One-man show in Quadriennale exhibition, Rome. Mussolini buys *Lady with a Veil* and *Ecce puer*, the very same works that Clemenceau had selected for the Luxembourg. Francesco Rosso institutes Premio Medardo Rosso at the Brera Academy.

1934 Private museum set up at Barzio (Valsassina) near Como.

1935 Included in exhibition of modern Italian art, Musée du Jeu de Paume, Paris.

1946 One-man show, Galleria Santo Spirito, Milan.

1950 One-man show, Venice Biennale.

1957 Included in exhibition of twentieth-century Italian art, Akademie der Künste, Berlin, and in *Rodin, ses collaborateurs et ses amis*, Musée Rodin, Paris.

1959 University of Nebraska buys *Jewish Boy*; the Museum of Modern Art, New York, buys the *Concierge* and *Bookmaker*. December 15—January 16, 1960: exhibition at Peridot Gallery, New York.

1961 Included in exhibition *Sources du XXme siècle*, Musée d'Art Moderne, Paris, and in *Salute to Italy*, loan exhibition at the Wadsworth Atheneum, Hartford, Connecticut.

1962 Included in exhibition *Europäische Kunst, 1912*, Wallraf-Richartz Museum, Cologne.

1963 September: one-man show, Museum of Modern Art, New York.

Selected Bibliography

WRITINGS BY ROSSO

1 Lettera a Clemenceau. *Gazzetta di Venezia* February 24, 1921.
2 Concepimento—Limite—Infinito. *L'Ambrosiano* (Milan) January 12, 1926.
  Reprinted in the monograph by Mino Borghi (bibl. 4), pp. 57—60.
  For other writings and statements by Rosso, see the bibliography in Borghi (bibl. 4), p. 74.

MONOGRAPHS

3 BARBANTINI, NINO. Medardo Rosso. Venice, Neri Pozza, 1950.
  Barbantini probably first met Rosso in 1914; he was also friendly with Etha Fles, from whom he may have gleaned information. Unfortunately, he wrote this monograph many years after Rosso's death.
4 BORGHI, MINO. Medardo Rosso. Milan, Ed. del Milione, 1950.
  Borghi, a disciple of the art historian Giorgio Nicodemi, the recently retired editor of *L'Arte*, worked closely with Francesco Rosso, who remembered a great deal of what his father had told him but did not have the training to seize the significant details, both because he was an industrialist and because he did not know the Paris his father reminisced about. The clippings and letters preserved by Rosso were analyzed, partly incorporated in the book, and listed chronologically in the bibliography. A confused yet essential monograph, it gives no life to Rosso's most creative period in Paris, the years 1889—97. Whether Rosso, because of his secretiveness, spoke little of this time or whether his son forgot what he was told remains an enigma. Rosso probably met his son between 1909 and 1911, some twenty years after he had left for Paris in 1889.
5 [BORGMEYER, CHARLES LOUIS. L'Oeuvre de Medardo Rosso. Venice, 1916.
  This book is listed among the monographs in the bibliography in Borghi (bibl. 4) and may perhaps come to light in manuscript when the Rosso papers at Barzio are re-examined. Borgmeyer wrote for the *Fine Arts Journal* (Chicago), to which, in 1914, he was contributing a series called "Among Sculptures." Mr. John Harthan, Keeper of the Library at the Victoria and Albert Museum, examined the files of the *Fine Arts Journal* for 1914 and subsequent years and reached the conclusion that the article was never published.]
6 COZZANI, ETTORE. Medardo Rosso. Milan, L'Eroica, 1931.
  A poetic apologia, it reveals a familiarity with the sculptor about whom the author had written as early as 1910.
7 FLES, ETHA. Medardo Rosso, der Mensch und der Künstler. Freiburg (Baden), Walter Heinrich, 1922.
  All Miss Fles's writings on Rosso are of interest because she knew him since 1900. However, her dates are not always reliable. For the relationship between Miss Fles and Rosso, see bibl. 20.
8 PAPINI, GIOVANNI. Medardo Rosso. Milan, Hoepli, 1945.
  A paper book containing fifteen pages of text by one of the three editors of *La Voce*, who must have known Rosso since 1910, if not earlier.
9 PIERARD LOUIS. Un sculpteur impressioniste, Medardo Rosso. Paris, Ed. de la Société Nouvelle, 1909. 7 pp. plus illus., bibliography taken from index in the Cremetti album (see bibl. 57).
  Piérard was a writer and poet who later became a Socialist deputy of Le Borinage in the Belgian Parliament and also wrote a book on van Gogh. Contains a few facts not recorded elsewhere. A rare booklet, photocopy in the library of the Museum of Modern Art, New York.
10 SOFFICI, ARDENGO. Medardo Rosso. Florence, Vallecchi, 1929.
  All the writings of Soffici are important because he was a painter writing about art and a critic who knew the Italian as well as the French scene. He was a great friend of Rosso's and writes about him with a sense of his stature as an artist and a full appreciation of his bizarre, quixotic personality. His anecdotes are delightful and sympathetically told. His campaign in *La Voce* was heroic in its persistence; it is no exaggeration to say that he and his co-editors Prezzolini and Papini are responsible for the re-evaluation of Rosso in Italy.

GENERAL WORKS AND ARTICLES

11 ADLOW, DOROTHY. The rediscovery of Rosso. *Christian Science Monitor* January 2, 1960.

12 AMBROSINI, LUIGI. Teocrito, Ariosto, minori e minimi. Milan, Corbaccio, 1926, pp. 355–68.
   Rosso's obiter dicta are assembled and made clear in these charming reminiscences.

13 APOLLINAIRE, GUILLAUME. Chroniques d'art: 1902–1918. Ed. L.-C. Breunig. Paris, Gallimard, 1960.

14 Archives bibliographiques contemporaines. Paris, 1906, I, pp. 69-71.
   The Rosso entry is very inexact and was inspired if not actually written by Etha Fles. It is reprinted in the Cremetti album, bibl. 57.

15 ASHTON, DORE. Art, the year's acquisitions. Modern Museum's exhibition covers range of styles from 1890 to present. *New York Times* December 4, 1959.

16 ASHTON, DORE. A sculptor of mystical feeling. *New York Times* December 27, 1959.

17 AUREL [MME MORTIER]. Rodin devant la femme; fragments inédits de Rodin. Sa technique par lui-même. Paris, Maison du Livre, 1919.

18 BARBANTINI, NINO. I moderni all'XI Biennale Veneziana, Medardo Rosso, James Ensor. *Vita d'Arte* v. 7 no. 80 August 1914.

19 BARR, MARGARET SCOLARI. Reviving Medardo Rosso. *Art News* v. 58 no. 9:36–38, 66–67 ill. January 1960.

20 BARR, MARGARET SCOLARI. Medardo Rosso and His Dutch Patroness Etha Fles. *Nederlands Kunsthistorisch Jaarboek* v. 13:217–51 ill. 1962.

21 BAUDELAIRE, CHARLES. The Mirror of Art. Tr. and ed. Jonathan Mayne. New York, Doubleday Anchor Books, 1956, pp. 119ff.

22 BOCCIONI, UMBERTO. Pittura, scultura futuriste. Milan, Edizioni futuriste di "Poesia," 1914.

23 CALVESI, MAURIZIO. Il futurismo di Boccioni; formazione e tempi. *Arte antica e moderna* no. 2: 149–69, April–June 1958.
   For Rosso's influence on Boccioni.

24 CARAMEL, LUCIANO. La prima attività di Medardo Rosso e i suoi rapporti con l'ambiente milanese. *Arte Lombarda* v. 6 no. 2 December 1961.

25 CARAMEL, LUCIANO. I "ritorni" di Medardo Rosso e due bronzi giovanili. *Commentari* v. 13 no. 3: 247–53, July–December 1962.

26 CARANDENTE, GIOVANNI. Rosso. Dictionary of Modern Sculpture. Ed. Robert Maillard. New York, Tudor, 1961.

27 CARRA, CARLO. La mia vita. Milan, Rizzoli, 1943.

28 CARRIERI, RAFFAELE. Il disegno italiano contemporaneo. Milan, Damiani, 1950.

29 CARRIERI, RAFFAELE. Pittura, scultura d'avanguardia in Italia, 1890–1950. Milan, Conchiglia, 1950.

30 CASSOU, JEAN. Panorama des arts plastiques contemporains. Paris, Gallimard, 1960.

31 CHIODO, MARIO VIANELLO. Medardo Rosso, nel primo anniversario. *Il Gazzettino* (Venice) March 31, 1929.

32 CHIODO, MARIO VIANELLO. Ricordo di Medardo Rosso. *La Biennale di Venezia* 3:27–28 January 1951.

33 CHIODO, MARIO VIANELLO. Medardo Rosso. *Ateneo Veneto* v. 142 no. 1 January–June 1958.

34 CLADEL, JUDITH. Rodin, sa vie glorieuse et inconnue. Paris, Grasset, 1936.
   For Rosso's influence on Rodin, see p. 243.

35 CLARIS, EDMOND. De l'impressionisme en sculpture. Paris, Ed. Nouvelle Revue Française, 1902.

36 CLOUGH, ROSA TRILLO. Futurism. New York, Philosophical Library, 1961.

37 COSTANTINI, VINCENZO. Scultura e pittura italiana contemporanea, 1880–1926. Milan, Hoepli, 1940.

38 COSTANTINI, VINCENZO. Architettura, scultura, pittura contemporanea europea in un secolo di materialismo. Milan, Ceschina, 1951.

39 CROCE, BENEDETTO and VOSSLER, KARL. Briefwechsel Benedetto Croce—Karl Vossler. Berlin-Frankfurt, Suhrkamp, 1951; Italian ed., 1951.

40 Editorial: Medardo Rosso 1858–1928. *Burlington Magazine* v. 92 no. 571:277–78, October 1950.

41 ELSEN, ALBERT E. Rodin. New York, The Museum of Modern Art, 1963.

42 FLES, ETHA. Medardo Rosso. *Elsevier's geillustreerd Maandschrift* (Amsterdam) v. 29 July–December 1919.

43 FLES, ETHA. Drie Visionnaire Kunstenaars van onzen Tijd; Medardo Rosso, Gerardo Dottori, Ernesto Masuelli. Haarlem, Enschedé, 1936.

44 GAMBILLO, MARIA DRUDI and FIORI, TERESA. Archivi del futurismo (Archivi dell'arte contemporanea, v. 1). Rome, De Luca, 1958, pp. 64, 69, 70, 178, 319.

45 GENAUER, EMILY. Experiments of the Present Form Our View of the Past. *New York Herald Tribune* December 20, 1959.

46 GIEDION-WELCKER, CAROLA. Contemporary Sculpture: An Evolution in Volume and Space. New York, Wittenborn, 1955.

47 GOLDSCHEIDER, CECILE. La genèse d'une oeuvre: Le Balzac de Rodin. *Revue des arts* v. 2 no. 1 March 1952.

48 GOLDSCHEIDER, CECILE. Rodin, sa vie, son oeuvre, son héritage. Paris, Les Productions de Paris, 1962–63.

49 GUBERNATIS, ANGELO DE. Dizionario degli artisti italiani viventi. Florence, 1889.

Incomplete but useful because it lists what Rosso showed in Venice in 1887.

50 HEVESY, LUDWIG. Medardo Rosso. *Kunst und Kunsthandwerk* (Vienna) v. 8:174—84 1905.

51 INGLESE, OSCAR. Medardo Rosso. *Commentari* v. 7 no. 2:110—21, April—June 1956.

52 KLEEHOVEN, H. A. VON. Medardo Rosso a Vienna. *La Biennale di Venezia* no. 23:23—25 January 1955.

53 KRAMER, HILTON. Medardo Rosso. *Arts* v. 34 no. 3:30—37 December 1957.

54 KUH, KATHARINE. Great Sculpture, A private Showing for SR Readers of the Hirshhorn Collection. *Saturday Review* v. 45 no. 6 pp. 14—21 June 23, 1962.

55 *Lacerba* (Florence). Ed. Giovanni Papini. 1913—15.

Contains references to Rosso only in the early numbers.

56 LAVAGNINO, EMILIO. L'arte moderna dai neoclassici ai contemporanei. Turin, UTET, 1961.

57 LONDON. EUGENE CREMETTI GALLERY. Medardo Rosso: Impressions. 1906.

Album published on the occasion of the exhibition.

58 MEIER-GRAEFE, JULIUS. Modern Art; being a contribution to a new system of aesthetics. Tr. from the German by Florence Simmonds and George W. Chrystal. 2 vols. London, William Heinemann, New York, Putnam's Sons, 1908, II, "Medardo Rosso," pp. 21—28, and "Impressionism in Sculpture," pp. 30—36.

59 MICHELI, MARIO DE. Scultura italiana del dopoguerra. Milan, Schwarz, 1958, pp. 266ff.

60 NEW YORK. GRAND CENTRAL ART GALLERIES. Exhibition of Modern Italian Art, Auspices of the Italy-America Society. 1926. Introduction by Arduino Colasanti, foreword by Christian Brinton.

61 NICODEMI, GIORGIO. Une "Epreuve Unique" della "Rieuse" e due disegni di Medardo Rosso. *L'Arte* v. 24 no. 4:375—78 October—December 1959.

62 PAPINI, GIOVANNI. Scrittori e artisti. Milan, Mondadori, 1959, pp. 1268ff.

63 PRESTON, STUART. New York Review. *Burlington Magazine* v. 102 no. 684:132 March 1960.

64 PREZZOLINI, GIUSEPPE. Il tempo della Voce. Milan-Florence, Longanesi-Vallecchi, 1960, pp. 267ff.

65 RITCHIE, ANDREW. Sculpture of the Twentieth Century. New York, The Museum of Modern Art, 1952, p. 17.

66 SEIDEL, CURT. L'arte di Medardo Rosso. *L'artista moderno* (Turin) v. 10 March 10, 1911.

67 SEUPHOR, MICHEL. The Sculpture of This Century. London, Zwemmer, 1959; New York, Braziller, 1960, pp. 20—24, 42, 324—25.

68 SEVERINI, GINO. Tutta la vita di un pittore. Cernusco sul Naviglio, Garzanti, 1946.

69 SOBY, JAMES THRALL and BARR, ALFRED H., JR. Twentieth-Century Italian Art. New York, The Museum of Modern Art, 1949, pp. 7, 13.

70 SCHIFF, BENNETT. In the Art Galleries. *New York Post* December 19, 1959.

71 SOFFICI, ARDENGO. Il caso Medardo Rosso, preceduto da l'impressionismo e la pittura italiana. Florence, Seeber, 1909.

72 SOFFICI, ARDENGO. Ricordi di vita artistica e letteraria. Florence, Vallecchi, 1942.

73 SOFFICI, ARDENGO. Trenta artisti moderni italiani e stranieri. Florence, Vallecchi, 1950.

74 SOMARE, ENRICO. La scultura di Medardo Rosso. *L'Esame* (Milan) v. 6 no. 1:3—25 March 1939.

75 TAYLOR, JOSHUA C. Futurism. New York, The Museum of Modern Art, 1961, pp. 17, 87, 92, 93, 120, 130—31.

76 LA VOCE (Florence). Ed. Giuseppe Prezzolini. 1908—16.

Contains articles on Medardo Rosso or references to him in practically every number.

Index

by Lucy R. Lippard

(Numbers in italics refer to illustrations; footnotes follow page references)

PHOTOGRAPH CREDITS

Bacci, Milan: p. 82 *right*; Oliver Baker: pp. 22, 24, 29 *right*, 33, 37, 44, 57, 79, 80; Gianni Berengo-Gardin, Venice: p. 51; Lee Boltin: *cover*; Clari, Milan: p. 41 *below*; Claudio Emmer, Milan: p. 35; Gabinetto Fotografico Nazionale, Rome: pp. 12 *left*, 20, 23, 27, 29 *left*, 32, 34, 42; Giacomelli, Venice: pp. 50, 52; R. Peter Petersen: pp. 13, 40, 45, 66; Walter Rosenblum: 31, 39; John Szarkowski: *frontispiece*; Vasari, Rome: p. 17.